This slender volume, like the ever modest giant it commemorates, is simple, and yet profound. The contributors are well known across the spectrum of world evangelicalism – not the sectarian politicized variety caught in the glare of a rightfully suspicious public press – but those who graciously, lovingly, and without fanfare follow their Lord in the irenic spirit of John Stott. This book reminds us that he exemplified as few public evangelical figures have the good news of "the depth of the riches of the wisdom and knowledge of God!" Every chapter in this book celebrates dimensions of Stott's character and work in ways that remind readers how to "be imitators of God as dearly loved children and live a life of love . . . ." (Eph 5:1–2). Those who read and ponder this book will find their spirits encouraged, their minds renewed, and their faith invigorated. I guarantee it.

Jonathan J. Bonk, PhD
Executive Director Emeritus,
Overseas Ministries Study Center, New Haven, Connecticut, USA
Research Professor of Mission,
Founding Director Emeritus, *Dictionary of African Christian Biography*,
Boston University, Massachusetts, USA

John Stott's influential work, *The Radical Disciple*, is the springboard for this collection of superb essays that extends and develops Stott's legacy. Most contributors knew Stott personally, and their memories reveal an authentic, compassionate, and humble Christian, who preferred "Uncle John" to any title. He inspired multifaceted reflection on social action as integral to God's mission in the world. This collection deepens and expands his efforts for social justice rooted in biblical preaching, so that the global church might be salt and light in a world torn by racial and ethnic strife and concerned for God's creation.

Jesus declared that "a student is not above the teacher, but everyone who is fully trained will be like their teacher" (Luke 6:40 NIV); these "students" of John Stott have proved their teacher's wisdom and modeled his passion for proclaiming God's full gospel of love and justice.

Lynn H. Cohick, PhD
Provost, Dean of Academic Affairs, and Professor of New Testament,
Northern Seminary, Lisle, Illinois, USA

One significant moment in my life was when (after the General Committee of IFES in Paris 1959) I met John Stott in Cambridge during a course that Inter-Varsity UK organized for a group of delegates. He was our guide in the visit to Cambridge and became one of my mentors. Through the years I could see how his mind grew with his experiences of ministering in numerous places around the world. I was his companion and translator in places such as Quito, Ecuador; Lima, Perú; Recife, Brasil; Córdoba, Argentina; Urbana, USA; and Toronto, Canada. His ministry was crucial in the development of the Lausanne movement around the world. I am glad and thankful for this book that reflects his lasting influence at a global level. Praise the Lord for John Stott.

J. Samuel Escobar, PhD
Emeritus Professor of Missiology,
Palmer Theological Seminary, Wynnewood, Pennsylvania, USA
President, United Bible Societies
Former President, International Fellowship of Evangelical Students

What a gift this book is! This volume brings together an exceptional group of international scholars to celebrate the life and work of one of the most important Christian thinkers of the recent past. John Stott's lifelong pursuit of an integrated Christian life that is centered on God and finds expression in relationships with others led him to work tirelessly for the inclusion and unity of all persons as image-bearers of God with a single-minded focus on service as the natural outflow of the Christian life. Stott's life and work will continue to transform Christian witness for generations to come – and *Living Radical Discipleship* bears witness to that.

George Kalantzis, PhD
Professor of Theology, Wheaton College, Illinois, USA
Director, The Wheaton Center for Early Christian Studies
Senior Fellow, International Association for Refugees (IAFR)

This book of reflections on the life and work of John R. W. Stott is both a tribute to his legacy and a live conversation on the theological themes that occupy us. The insightful talks and remembrances are themselves a testament, not just to his continuing intellectual influence, but to the depth of his friendships and the breadth of his concern for the global church.

I was one of those who took shelter under his giant shadow when as a young woman my early writings four decades ago on culture, gospel and society roused much heat and misunderstanding. Without the cognitive support and encouragement of leaders like him, I would not have had the courage and stamina to continue. John Stott's humble readiness to listen and come alongside Majority World people birthing new wineskins was rare among leaders of his time. This book is a rich treasure of his iconic impact as an inspiring and radical disciple of our Lord Christ.

Melba Padilla Maggay, PhD
President,
Institute for Studies in Asian Church and Culture

Arguably, no other evangelical leader has had more influence in shaping global evangelicalism in the twentieth and twenty-first centuries than the Englishman, John R. W. Stott. His life and legacy as a clergyman, scholar, evangelist, writer, and shaper of movements and institutions has impacted leaders young and old on every continent. An endowed chair in his honor in the Human Needs and Global Resources (HNGR) Program at Wheaton College perfectly symbolizes, as an eternal reminder, this man's contribution to the global church.

The Fall Symposium of the HNGR program at Wheaton in 2019 was aptly themed from the final book Stott wrote, *The Radical Disciple: Some Neglected Aspects of Our Calling*. This compendium demonstrates in a clear way the incarnational and transformative power of the gospel as John Stott experienced personally, lived out in his clerical parish, and taught in his amazing corpus of theological writings. Each chapter's critical reflections on what being a radical disciple of Christ means show not only the influence Stott had on the writer's life and work but also how in today's society we can be a radical disciple, loving Jesus in all of life.

I find this book truly provocative, stimulating, and inspiring. This is a visionary challenge of what the gospel can achieve in personal and community life.

Las G. Newman, PhD
Global Associate Director for Regions,
Lausanne Movement

These essays – some more anecdotal, but all theologically perceptive – are more than a fitting tribute to John Stott's memory and legacy. They embody his lifelong commitment to a discipleship of mind and heart, radical faith and just works. As such, they present a powerful challenge to our complacency, shameful compromises, and meaningless polarizations. This is a book to be pondered by all who care for the credibility of the church in our contemporary world.

Vinoth Ramachandra, PhD
International Secretary for Dialogue and Social Engagement,
International Fellowship of Evangelical Students

This book is an excellent introduction and faithful response to radical discipleship preached and lived by John Stott! Sadly, his call for a double listening both to the word and to the world has become rather a bigger challenge due to the privatization of faith which is lost in the public square. I am sure dear Uncle John would be pleased to recommend this global collaboration of his dear friends. Every contributor goes further in grasping the radicalness of the good news for the whole world instead of repeating clichés of congratulations. As a publisher who has translated and published forty titles by John Stott, I heartily recommend *Living Radical Discipleship: Inspired by John Stott* to the global Christians living between and in two worlds, especially to the young generation, for the formation of radical discipleship.

Hyoun-Ki Shin
Publisher, Korea InterVarsity Press

This Stott Symposium volume has probing reflections on costly, uncompromising discipleship by global leaders shaped and nurtured by the amazing life and ministry of John Stott. These penetrating essays from all parts of the global church help us understand more clearly how to apply the gospel to every area of life.

Ronald J. Sider, PhD
Distinguished Professor Emeritus, Theology, Holistic Ministry and Public Policy,
Palmer Seminary at Eastern University, St David's, Pennsylvania, USA

The church needs a thoughtful relevant guide to become a community that reflects God's kingdom. This book is a critical resource for reflective practitioners and practical theologians who desire biblically grounded and socially informed ways forward to living in this world as the body of Christ. You will find yourself considering the intersections of witness, economic justice, environmental stewardship, and how the gospel empowers us to respond in courage. This global collection of scholar neighbors will awaken us to questions we need to be asking and provide frameworks for how the gospel invites us to be engaged citizens.

Rev. Sandra Van Opstal
Founding Director, Chasing Justice
Author, *The Next Worship*

Living Radical Discipleship

Langham
GLOBAL LIBRARY

Living Radical Discipleship

Inspired by John Stott

Edited by

Laura S. Meitzner Yoder

GLOBAL LIBRARY

Published 2021 by Langham Global Library
An imprint of Langham Publishing
www.langhampublishing.org

Langham Publishing and its imprints are a ministry of Langham Partnership

Langham Partnership
PO Box 296, Carlisle, Cumbria, CA3 9WZ, UK
www.langham.org

ISBNs:
978-1-83973-071-9 Print
978-1-83973-107-5 ePub
978-1-83973-108-2 Mobi
978-1-83973-109-9 PDF

British Library Cataloguing-in-Publication Data
A catalogue record for this book is available from the British Library.

ISBN: 978-1-83973-071-9

Cover & Book Design: projectluz.com

Featured cover image is a mosaic designed by Rachel Hammitt.

The Human Needs and Global Resources Program logo on the cover represents growth and rootedness, as well as flourishing and unity. The tree and the circle are deeply symbolic as individual components, but when joined together, they embody the values the Program stands for, namely, "a life-orienting commitment to justice, intercultural humility, compassion, hospitality, environmental health, and peacemaking, as actively reflected in lifestyle and vocation."

Rachel Hammitt, Logo Designer

Contents

Foreword

One of the privileges of the work I do is that I get to meet and collaborate with all sorts of people, and often those people become friends. Laura Meitzner Yoder is one such person. We have met only a few times, but I know she is a kindred spirit, and so I was delighted when she asked me to pen some opening words for this book. I never met John Stott, but I read his books as a young Theology undergraduate and am well aware that so much of what I stand for now demonstrates the long shadow of his legacy.

John Stott was a remarkable man – one who sought to listen as well as speak; to learn as well as teach; and who was prepared to change as well as seeking to stay constantly faithful to and rooted in his Saviour, Jesus Christ. It is fitting, therefore, that this is a remarkable book, and I have been changed through reading it, with each chapter giving me a nugget to chew on.

I rejoiced with Laura over the beauty of Oecusse and grieved the tragedy of human stupidity. From Bishop Zac Niringiye I have been reflecting on the nature of citizenship and where my privilege has blinded me. Chris Wright challenged me again that the power and heart of the church is not in the US or the UK, and that we who live there need to put our egos away and draw from those who are located at the geographical heart of Christianity. Myrto Theocharous stunned me with her brilliance in moving the focus of the image of God from the receiver to the giver (I nearly got there in my writing on the image of God in *Saying Yes to Life*, but she made the final jump).

From Ruth Padilla DeBorst I have been thinking about the power of community and what it means for radical discipleship to take place with our roots entwined with those of others. Kuki Rokhum re-envisioned me on the central role of the church: if we want to bring change, we need to equip and educate the church. I have been prompted by Jason Fileta to consider whether I treat justice as a project or whether it is deeply ingrained in my life. And Mark Labberton inspired me afresh with his insights into John Stott's life and the powerful inspiration he still gives us. Oh, if I could be but a fraction of the Christ-centred person Stott was!

You will no doubt discover your own nuggets in these chapters. Please don't read this book if you only want your brain tickled (though that will happen).

Please read this book to be stirred and challenged and called to deeper action for God's kingdom.

In my work with Tearfund I am faced daily with the groans of creation, emanating from both people and the wider natural world. All around the globe we are living with social and environmental disaster, and yet our churches continue to be preoccupied with personal salvation and evangelism. I am still utterly committed to both those things, but on their own they give us an emaciated gospel, not the full gospel of justice, righteousness and reconciliation for which Jesus came.

That full, integrated gospel demands a radical response from us – in how we live personally and together in our churches. I pray that the words of this book will move us to act justly, love mercy and to walk humbly with our God.

Ruth Valerio

Preface

Laura S. Meitzner Yoder

Prominent in John Stott's evangelical message is his insistence, sometimes bluntly stated, that faith commitments must be evident in the everyday lives of Christ's followers. In his final book, *The Radical Disciple: Some Neglected Aspects of Our Calling*, rather than reprise the theological core which he had developed in his best-known writings, Stott focuses on eight elements that he deemed underemphasized, absent, or muted in the lived-out testimonies of many believers. His selection which includes chapters on nonconformity, creation care, simplicity, balance, Christlikeness, maturity, dependence, and death may seem eclectic or mundane for a deliberately final work.

However, naming a wide-ranging array of elements is not surprising when we recall that Stott is always forthright about discipleship as embracing the all-encompassing lordship of Christ. He writes, "My concern . . . is that we who claim to be disciples of the Lord Jesus will provoke him to say again, 'Why do you call me, "Lord, Lord," and do not do what I say?' (Luke 6:46)."[1] "Our common way of avoiding radical discipleship is to be selective: choosing those areas in which commitment suits us and staying away from those areas in which it will be costly. But because Jesus is Lord, we have no right to pick and choose the areas in which we will submit to his authority."[2]

We do pick and choose. Ignoring creation care, avoiding risky social engagement, and failing to see or to hear people who have been marginalized are three areas of disobedience we commonly practice and justify in all kinds of ways. For Stott, evidence of Christian commitment should be visible through the disciple's everyday actions and behaviour. He often said, "Pretty songs . . . don't prove anything. It's only in daily life that you prove, through obedience, whether or not you love Jesus."[3]

To reflect on integral radical discipleship together, the authors in this book – many scholar-practitioner church leaders who knew John Stott well

---

1. Stott, *Radical Disciple*, 14–15.

2. Stott, 15–16.

3. Quoted in Christopher J. H. Wright, *Portraits of a Radical Disciple: Recollections of John Stott's Life and Ministry*, 239.

and worked with him across decades of his ministry – gathered for a special Symposium, convened by the Human Needs and Global Resources Program at Wheaton College with substantial involvement from faculty and staff across campus, on 6–8 October 2019.

Many convictions evident in John Stott's ministry are mirrored in the Human Needs and Global Resources Program. Stott distinctively held together his sharing the good news of Jesus Christ through biblical teaching and preaching with his understanding that social action is integral to the life of discipleship. These convictions regarding creation care, social engagement, and advocating for recognition of and investment in Majority World church leadership deepened over the course of his life and ministry. They were anchored in Stott's unwavering insistence that we recognize the fully transformative reality of the lordship of Christ over all of creation and in every aspect of a Christian's life.

Notably, Stott's commitments extended to substantial and long-standing involvement in multiple institutions that reflected his understanding of integral mission and for which his theological contributions were formative. The 2019 Symposium highlighted three organizations that exemplify Stott's enduring affiliations:

- The *Langham Partnership*, founded by Stott in 1969 and funded by income from his books and speaking honoraria, grew out of his profound commitment to supporting global church leadership by developing resources and supporting theological education and biblical training for pastors.
- *Tearfund* has joined compassion with practical action since 1968, serving as a leading evangelical voice in Christian social engagement. Tearfund equips and mobilizes local churches and other organizations to support communities working to overcome poverty, violence, and disasters. Stott served as Tearfund president from 1983–1997.
- *A Rocha* engages and equips Christians in twenty countries to deepen their connection to God through the active care of creation. A committed birdwatcher, Stott served on A Rocha's Council of Reference from their 1983 founding to the end of his life, and he informed and inspired A Rocha's theological framework.

The authors of this volume collectively remind us that Christian obedience necessarily includes caring for God's creation, engaging in social action and advocacy, and repenting from our draw to power as we are attentive to people who have been marginalized. While the chapters are grouped according to emphasis, these themes are as intertwined in these contributions as they were in Stott's life. Mark Labberton offers an opening reflection on how the gospel took hold of Stott's life, and how this transformation was evident in many dimensions of his theological formation, relationships, and lifestyle. Chris Wright describes Stott's vision for equipping Majority World church leaders in order to strengthen the church worldwide.

Reflecting on Christian social engagement, Myrto Theocharous reframes being the image of God as enacting the divine task of justice: "being aware that I am responsible for the life of the other." Challenging us to hear the gospel story from contexts of marginalization, oppression, and exploitation, Zac Niringiye urges us to exercise gospel obedience in the public square. Jason Fileta contrasts the inadequacy of "justice as a project" to the relentless love of Jesus's compassion that leads to a whole, integrated life orientation toward just living and action.

The final section conveys how Stott envisioned caring for creation as beginning with God, not with humanity. Ruth Padilla DeBorst invites us to see the webs of interconnection among people and other creatures, and to humbly listen to the Spirit's pleading and leading on our relationships with the rest of God's created order. As Kuki Rokhum narrates her own growing understanding of integral mission, she discusses the practical challenges and new orientations for the church in India and worldwide on loving God and caring for all who depend on God's good creation. My concluding chapter explores how we come to recognize our effects on God's world, with glimpses of this process in colonial environmental history, inequitable water access in a remote island enclave, and John Stott's own growing environmental concern that was nurtured by his biblical convictions alongside increased direct awareness of everyday suffering experienced in the Majority World regions through Christian leaders he came to know.

You are invited to consider and to act boldly together on these experiences and reflections about lived-out radical discipleship – in the life of John Stott, the commitments of these church leaders, and the life testimonies of disciples worldwide seeking earnestly to follow the Way, the Truth, and the Life.

References

Stott, John. *The Radical Disciple: Some Neglected Aspects of Our Calling*. Downers Grove, IL: InterVarsity Press, 2010.

Wright, Christopher J. H., ed. *Portraits of a Radical Disciple: Recollections of John Stott's Life and Ministry*. Downers Grove, IL: InterVarsity Press, 2011.

Acknowledgments

The Symposium that led to this collection was also a celebration. In 2013, friends of Wheaton College established an endowment in John Stott's name for the Human Needs and Global Resources Program, which since 1976 has facilitated learning from Majority World leaders how the global church understands needs in their midst and beyond, and mobilizes their God-given resources to address them. This Stott endowment substantially increases affordability for student interns and makes possible many new initiatives that broaden the Program's impact on Wheaton College's campus and beyond. We give thanks to God for the many and varied good fruits that this generous gift has already yielded in its initial years.

The October 2019 Symposium featured a wide variety of people whose work has been made possible and enhanced in varied ways through this endowment: International Visiting Scholars who spent a term at Wheaton College engaging the campus and regional communities; Wheaton faculty who took a dedicated study/research leave semester to live in the Majority World, focusing on global Christian responses to critical human needs; scholars who received research and creative project grants to compose music, to conduct innovative fieldwork, and to synthesize their project results; and faculty who supervised independent research or creative projects of Human Needs and Global Resources student interns, and then went on to publish and to disseminate their outcomes. This event also included the inaugural lecture of the John Stott Endowed Chair in Human Needs and Global Resources, included here as my final chapter, which also featured two exquisite performances by composer Shawn Okpebholo, pianist Karin Edwards, and vocalist Joelle LaMarre.

The Symposium and this book project would not have been possible without the keen interest and unflagging support of many people, especially my spectacular colleagues in the Human Needs and Global Resources Program: Laura Atkinson, Mandy Kellums Baraka, Corrie Johnson, Alex Jones, Rachel Hammitt, Nina Mantalaba, and notably Jamie Huff for overseeing the Symposium event. Special thanks are due to each of the contributing authors and to those who reviewed the manuscript and wrote endorsements; to faculty colleagues who hosted various aspects of the Symposium; to Margaret Diddams and Laura Montgomery for initial co-visioning of this project and ongoing interest; to Rusty Pritchard, David Jones, Lynn Cohick, George Kalantzis, Peter Harris, Dave Bookless, Sarah Stanley, David McNutt, and Mary and Dennis Bambury who gave formative feedback at key times; to Crystal Downing and David Downing who hosted a roundtable on Christian publishing at the Wade Center; Mark Purcell of A Rocha and Wesley Crawford for leading in worship and a creative workshop; many friends and colleagues at Tearfund and Tearfund USA; and to Vivian Doub at Langham for her encouragement in seeing this through to production.

The mosaic featured on the cover was based on the Human Needs and Global Resources Program logo, designed by Rachel Hammitt. In 2018 Wheaton College Community Art professor Leah Samuelson created this mosaic with students Sam Beattie, Alice Gorman, Miles Lindholz, and Gretta Swanson as a class project. Samuelson likens the repetitive work of setting tesserae in fresh mortar to the everyday life of discipleship: "Each tessera on its own could be seen as mundane, but when cut individually with great care and placed into a larger design, thousands of small, faithful actions create a beautiful image."

Final thanks go to Jeff and to Micah for your accompaniment and for brightening each and every day!

Laura Meitzner Yoder
Wheaton, September 2020

Part 1

Commitment to Majority World Church Leadership

1

Between Two Worlds?

The Gospel in the Life of John Stott

Mark Labberton

Just to be clear: only God knows what the gospel in the life of Rev Dr John R. W. Stott actually was. Here I consider the life of John Stott through an unapologetically personal lens, offering not a hagiography, nor an attempt to try to make him either more or less than he was. Rather I try to describe as simply and clearly as I can the person I actually experienced John to be. When we come to know people, especially well-known people, they often become less impressive the more we know them. For me, John was the opposite: the more I came to know him, the more impressive he became. I offer here an outline of a few core aspects of how the gospel took hold in John's life. I do so in the hope that Christians today may better reflect upon John's life and what it can mean to be a radical disciple of Jesus Christ.

Culturally Privileged

Everyone's story begins in the world into which they are born. In John Stott's case, that was into an upper-class English medical family who lived in a five-storey Georgian mansion on Harley Street in London's West End. It was a world of privilege, of elite, of private, boarding-school education from eight years of age. It was a world of manners, social place and intellectual achievement, lived out through the fears and brutalities of the Second World War, and in what turned out to be the closing decades of the British colonies. How was it that the reality of the gospel could so intersect with this privileged life that

3

John Stott could be profoundly transformed, not just morally or spiritually, theologically or intellectually, but culturally? How could a person born in this esteemed, formal, beautiful, economically and scientifically elite culture become someone who was so conformed to the image of Jesus over the course of his life? This is not a common narrative.

John's father was not only a highly respected physician, but later became the head of the Royal College of Surgeons during the Second World War. He had great expectations of his children, especially of his one son. John and his sisters were sent to elite schools, and it was while John was at Rugby School that E. J. H. Nash (a travelling evangelist with Scripture Union who was known as Bash) so preached the gospel in John's school chapel service that seventeen-year-old John made his own late-night, personal confession of faith, and put his trust in Christ. By that time, John had been in boarding school since he was eight years old, an experience of the classic English stereotype which, for John, reflected a cruel vestige of Victorian England. John felt sure that his upbringing in boarding schools, for all of its privilege, had left a negative mark on his life from his experience of the forms of emotional and physical torment that accompanied such settings. Meanwhile, Bash knew that every British prime minister had graduated from one of the top ten private schools in England, and that to bring such boys to Christ might change the face of England. John was one of many for whom privilege and proclamation converged in a deep and sustained conversion.

This was the beginning of a story of profound gospel change. To understand the gospel in John's life, we do best to begin by realizing it was a gospel that landed in a culturally privileged place. The gospel always meets us in our cultural location, whatever it may be, and the gospel seeks to redefine the social and cultural horizons of our lives as we are drawn out beyond them and into the new humanity for which we are being transformed by Jesus Christ. This was one of the most powerful ways in which John's life came to bear witness to God's surprising story.

Christ-Centred and Personally Discipled

The next thing about the gospel in John Stott's life is that his became a Christ-centred life. This was not just theologically true, but it became personally and transformatively true. The gospel that John received from the evangelist Bash was one that focused almost exclusively on the New Testament.

In the sermon in 1938 by which John came to faith, Bash preached on Revelation 3:20, which begins, "Behold, I stand at the door and knock." It was that sermon on that text that led John to come to a place where he was prepared to make a very deep and personal response to Christ. Fifty years later, John described it this way:

> Here, then, is the crucial question . . . : Have we ever opened our door to Christ? Have we ever [actually] invited him in? This was exactly the question which I needed to have put to me. For, intellectually speaking, I had believed in Jesus all my life, on the other side of the door. I had regularly struggled to say my prayers through the key-hole. I had even pushed pennies under the door in a vain attempt to pacify him. I had been baptized, yes and confirmed as well. I went to church, read my Bible, had high ideals and tried to be good and do good. But all the time, often without realizing it, I was actually holding Christ at arm's length and keeping him outside. I knew that to open the door might have momentous consequences. I am profoundly grateful to him for enabling me to open the door. Looking back now over more than fifty years, I realise that that simple step has changed the entire direction, course and quality of my life.[1]

Oh, that every disciple would be able to say that the way we heard, understood and responded to the gospel ultimately transformed us entirely and thoroughly!

The gospel that John received was not a gospel for a punctiliar kind of need, or for help with occasional anxiety, or for a hope of eternal life. It was a pervasive, gripping, transformative gospel, which only built in the life of John Stott. In part, this was due to the fact that Bash was a mentor in addition to being an evangelist. This explains why Bash wrote a multi-page handwritten letter to John every week for the next five years, teaching John what it meant to be a disciple. These were extraordinary letters of a discipling leader helping a young man emerge into adulthood, but even more, into maturity in Christ. Bash wanted to do what he could to help him consider all of the implications of the gospel in any and every aspect of life. John Stott emerged as he did through university and theological college because of the kind of deep personal discipleship that was part of the gospel he received.

Everything in John's life was about going deeper in Christ, wider in Christ, further in Christ. It was that kind of christological centre that drove everything about how John saw the world. Jesus was not just a confessional affirmation for the sake of an individual, interior conversion, but rather the centre of an

---

1. Cited in Dudley-Smith, *Making of a Leader*, 95.

entirely new lens on all of reality. For Bash, as for John, there was nothing about life that was outside the bounds of the lordship of Jesus. This was a remarkable affirmation, and I think it took root and gradually redefined John's social location. As he grew in his study of the Scriptures and in his experience in Christ, the call of the gospel was comprehensive enough to grab John's exceptionally keen mind and genuinely compassionate heart to rewrite the life of a person like him. Christ was John's cornerstone.

Many years later, in addition to many other things that he'd written, John wrote a regular column for *Christianity Today* under the title "Christ the Cornerstone." Consistently across all thirty-plus articles on widely varying topics is the primary concern for where Jesus Christ instructs us, leads us, motivates us, inspires us, challenges us, reorders us. The profundity of this pervasive Christocentric conviction defined John's faith, expressed and embodied across all of his life and ministry. He may have been born into life on Harley Street, but he was reborn into life in Christ.

Biblically Disciplined

John never wanted to say more or less than what he believed the Scriptures to teach. Eisegesis was not his game. He was always trying to knit together what the biblical text teaches us and the real connections to the world. This is what he referred to as living "between two worlds." He was gripped by the sense that this kind of biblical engagement could change our minds and our perceptions, both about the Bible and about the world we inhabit. This is God's gift in order that we might become different people, if only we will allow the rather covert work of the Bible to fully pervade our way of thinking.

One of John's favourite quotes was some marvellous words from Spurgeon in which he talks about the ways the preacher should prod the text, poke the text, study the text and consume the text, until eventually you lie down in the text and let the text soak into you so that your very blood becomes Bibline. That was Spurgeon – but it could have been John. The way John approached the biblical text embodied this incredible sense of wanting his very being to be pervaded by the Scriptures. By contrast, it seems that many seek spiritual experience that is spontaneous and personal, often entirely free from the Bible itself, and yet this is considered a singular mark of the presence of God in many communities of faith. I am moved by how significantly John's life was consciously bounded and disciplined by the Bible. He did not see it as a kind of straightjacket; rather, as a disciple he received the Bible's teaching as a staking out of the terrain within which we find our greatest freedom, our fullest humanity, our deepest love and our greatest compassion. John's interaction with Scripture was not a kind of doctrinaire approach to the Bible. *Between Two Worlds*, his book on preaching, underscored that preachers should commit themselves to the text of the biblical world and the contemporary world, and to the interpretive task of considering how these two things should be brought together. This is the work not merely of the preacher, but of all faithful, serious Christians.

In John's preaching, there was no tool or source from which he quoted more than the Bible. This was not because of a wooden biblicism; it was rather that he wanted to give his hearers the best food possible. For John that meant giving his hearers God's food through God's Word in order to nourish, sustain and change us.

Theologically Integrated

For John Stott, the gospel was here to change all of life. As John developed theologically, and as his grasp of the greater world extended outside the elite context in which he was raised, he came to see ever more fully the comprehensive nature and scope of the gospel. It is easy to imagine the effects of growing up in the early to mid-twentieth century in which the sun never set on the British Empire. It would be easily imaginable that "being English" in that time and place could constrain someone to see the world only through colonial eyes. After all, the first half of John's life had passed by before British colonialism actually began to be truly dismantled.

John's maturing faith led him to know and to understand the One who is Lord of all, not a mere king or queen. The One who is Lord sees and knows the whole compass. And the One who sees and knows the whole compass rules with justice: only with justice, only with love, only with mercy, only with an understanding of the full integrity, value and dignity of every human being throughout the whole world. This theocentric vision outstrips culture, class and status.

John recounted his emerging decolonializing vision of the world as he came to see that the gospel was for the whole world, not as a form of colonial tyranny, but as the source of life itself. John admitted that at the beginning of his discipleship he saw the gospel largely through colonial extensions, from the West to the Rest. But over time his theological vision began to change through Scripture and through his own experience. After he published *Basic Christianity*, John began to receive many invitations to speak around the world. Although these connections were naturally extensions of the culture and world in which English was primary, these relationships with Majority World Christians eventually challenged and changed him. For John, being theologically integrated must be a global reality lived out in every dimension of life and in all parts of the world. The claim that "Jesus is Lord" pertains to both the spiritual and the physical, about what is near and what is far, about what is internal and what is public. No dimension of life can be cordoned off from the reality of the gospel.

No doubt living in London shaped John in important ways: it was the dominating city of the world. That began to change in the mid to late twentieth century after the Second World War, but at the time when John was emerging as a young adult, London was still the centre. It turns out that Harley Street is in the parish of All Souls Church, Langham Place. The parish in which John was raised was the parish in which he served for the rest of his life. That parish is divided into two significantly different economic sections: one is upper class and the other is very low economically. It was in that context that John volunteered as a child to serve the homeless and the poor, out of a tender and sensitive conscience and a desire to be of help. These very young days in his life already bore the marks of John's compassion and vision that stretched his social context. As the gospel did its transformative work, these instincts only grew and deepened. The world was far bigger than life on Harley Street, and the gospel encompasses and seeks the welfare of all.

Eventually another factor came along that continued John's transformation, as it did for millions around the globe: the Second World War. Although John's father was the head of the Royal College of Surgeons during the war, John was convinced that his relatively new faith was leading him to become a pacifist. Imagine being a pacifist in the home of a father who is the head of the Royal College of Surgeons in the middle of the Second World War! At one point, John's father decided not to talk to him for a long, long time. Imagine the formative impact on John who, as an emerging young adult, was learning that the choice to be a follower of Christ might bring him into complete collision with the very family and background that gave him such privilege. It was clear early on to John that to follow Jesus meant reconsidering everything in light of Christ. He later gave up his pacifism, but only when that too became its own step of radical discipleship.

When people met John Stott, it was common for them to be impressed with his gracious manner, his English demeanour, the beauty of his voice and the gentleness of his spirit. These characteristics didn't convey what one might think of as a picture of radical discipleship. Yet at the core he lived out a radical faith and tenacity. It was a commitment. For John, there was a sense that discipleship in response to the gospel of Jesus Christ is a coherent whole for all our ordinary lives, and in all contexts. He was not a clericalist, but he was somebody who was committed to education, thoughtful formation, and certainly theological formation for people of every role and service in society. His interest in biblical, theological formation being needed by the church at large was not just about how we train people to be clergy or for standard forms of Christian ministry, but was for all Christian people in any dimension of life, who simply need to let the teaching and authority of the Scriptures pervade their life in every dimension.

Prayerfully Grounded

You did not have to be with John very long before realizing that prayer would be a key part of the discipline of your fellowship together. As one of his study assistants, I was particularly aware of this a number of times when travelling together, and in various circumstances where we would just naturally be brought together in prayer. A memorable and telling instance of this occurred when we went to a remote Christian camp in India. I arrived at 3 a.m., after John had already arrived. After some discussion, I eventually convinced the night guard to let me into the Quonset hut where John and I were to stay that week. It was a simple structure with a concrete floor and a metal roof. When I got in and found my bed, I saw John stirring a little in the shadows. He then did what I often saw him do when we were in a shared room – he pulled his legs up so that his knees were under him. So began his day: in prayer. Seeing that visibly played out in all the circumstances and places where we had opportunities to travel was something I found very moving. More poignantly, I think he is the only preacher I know who literally prepared sermons on his knees in prayer. Why was he unique in that? For John, reason, argument and persuasion all mattered, but he was convinced that the power of prayer was fundamental, both for the preacher and for the hearer.

Ecclesially Rooted

John also remained ecclesially rooted. He never saw himself as an independent agent, not even after he stepped down as rector of All Souls. It could have been easy for him to just be on his own, but he was always grounded in a community of people to whom he was accountable. He was accountable to a board, to a church, to a rector, to many. He saw his life in that way, and yet it was not a clubby kind of ecclesiology. He was one of the people who was a leader in establishing an evangelical Anglican church, not as a separate denomination, but inside the Church of England. He was deeply committed to the church – not just his church, but to the whole church. When he travelled and when he served he wanted to be with the church, he wanted to serve the church, he wanted to better understand what it would mean to serve the church.

Rationally Exacting

John was a man of reason with a very fine mind, and he wanted everyone else to be like him in that way. At least, he gently and sometimes insistently and quietly urged others to remember that reason should be given its due place. This was an area in which I differed from John, since I have less trust in rationality than John did. I shared his belief in the value and importance of reason, but not in its capacity or centrality in most people's lives. Reasoned clarity was one of the marks of John's understanding of the gospel, and one of the most valued marks of his teaching and writing.

Evangelistically Committed

John believed that the saving gospel of Jesus Christ should land in people's lives, and he believed that the saving gospel was a transformative gospel. If it landed, it would make a claim on the whole of life. His gospel was not a thin-ended gospel, a small interruption wedged into life. Instead it was his pervasive conviction that you preach the gospel in season and out of season, because we believe that in fact as we do so it will be transformative.

One story exemplified John's evangelistic tenacity. Many years ago, the *New York Times* journalist David Brooks wrote a column about John as a different kind of evangelical exemplar from most who were widely discussed in the American press.[2] Though the article was highly complimentary of John, it was not this that mattered to John himself. Instead what he wondered about was where David Brooks stood with Christ. So John wrote a thank-you note to David and invited him to meet him the next time they were in the same city. I remember John telling me that he and David were going to meet, and that with John's evangelistic courage and unqualified assertiveness, he was going to invite David to follow Jesus. I remember being struck by John's forwardness, and I wasn't sure this would be the best strategy at a first meeting with someone like David Brooks.

---

2. Brooks, "Who Is John Stott?"

Fast-forward to many years later, and I was in a setting where I myself was getting personally acquainted with David Brooks. At this point I didn't know what David Brooks thought of his meeting with John, though David's own spiritual journey was increasingly public. David said to me, "I understand that you knew John Stott." I wasn't sure where the conversation might go at this point. He then said, "You know, I had lunch with him."

"Yes," I replied. "Tell me about that."

So David began to tell me exactly what John had said. As far as I am aware, John never knew the impact of that lunch as one of the more powerful and influential conversations in David Brooks's life. In part, the journey that David Brooks is on to this day is a journey that was influenced by the courage and tenacity of John Stott's evangelistic life. John was consistently more interested in the gospel in someone's life than in any accolades for his own.

Colonially Repentant

Another quality of the gospel in John Stott's life was that he was colonially repentant. I mentioned this above, but as the cross at the centre of John's Christology grew in all of its implications, he became more and more aware of the way that the cross itself stood in judgment and in hope over any and every other form of power and authority. As a consequence, it really meant reshaping the political and social architecture of the world in which he had been nurtured, the world from which he had benefited. He came to see clearly that the world in which he lived and from which he benefited was profoundly distorting God's creation, bringing suffering and injustice, with a pervasive sense of crisis that was actually brought on by habits of Christian empire. All of that, in John's mind, had to be deeply reconsidered. The more he thought about the significance of the cross of Christ, the more sure he was that the cross was central to bringing to an end all forms of death, injustice and sin.

Relationally Transformed

After John wrote *Basic Christianity*, he carried out more and more university evangelistic missions in the Western world, and then gradually in various places in the Global South. His relationships with Christian leaders began to undo and redefine his sociology. Many of the people he began to meet had nothing in common with his privileged background, and, as relationships deepened, John was remade by the vivid, intelligent, costly discipleship lived by many in the Majority World. Among these were people who were among the greatest witnesses to the gospel in the twentieth century. This was a subtle but pervasive process of humbling change for John.

Often, these brothers and sisters were without material resources, without the privilege that had shaped and guided his life. Yet John saw them as people who were as intelligent and faithful as any he could imagine. Their circumstances and their vision of the world, alongside their understanding of the gospel, gradually unmasked and unravelled the sociology of John's own background. This process probably began in the 1960s and 70s, and it pervaded the rest of his life. Certainly some of the people that I heard John speak about the most were people who came from the Majority World, whose lives, vision and understanding of what it means to be a faithful disciple were remarkably different from his own.

John gave his life in part to travel, teaching, writing and scholarships, for the sake of the global church. He focused his energies on providing opportunities that allowed the voices of people in Majority World settings to come to the fore, to be heard, to have the full credibility that they deserved – a conviction that ironically and painfully is still not true of some parts of the evangelical movement. This, in part, explains why the first Lausanne Conference on World Evangelization became such an incredible turning point in global evangelicalism. The Lausanne Covenant, which John principally authored, became a significant document in part because of the way John's relationships of deep trust and mutual respect enabled him to write it in such a way that these profound voices could be heard. For John, these relationships redefined his vision of the world.

It was partly his time in the Global South that led John to maintain a very simple lifestyle. I remember one time when John wanted to have a new camera for bird photography, but he was troubled by the expense compared to the resources of so many others in the world. He just wanted a better camera. But John had a very sensitive conscience about spending any money that could otherwise go to some other and better purpose. Why would he struggle that way? He struggled that way because he had come to see, empathize and engage with issues of poverty and of privilege in ways he would not otherwise have done. This was a radical disconnection from his background and a very significant part of his own gospel transformation.

Globally Awakened

John's vision of the gospel and his friendships with the global church reset his social location. This is why I was most interested in working as his study assistant when I was invited to serve in that role. I wanted to understand how John had been formed, because it was clear that he had come from a particular social universe, but now his life, his vision, his activity, and even more his heart and mind, had been reset by deep friendships that extended out into the world at such a significant level that his own heart had been transformed by them.

So much of John's impact today can go back to his being globally awakened, and to his understanding of how the gospel calls us to respond to people. Early on in John's ministry, I remember being moved by his attentiveness to every Majority World Christian leader who reached out to him. Many letters came his way every day, but John's response was always personal. He listened and he wanted to serve. He wanted his personal resources, his own scholarship, his travel, his time, his royalties, to be of some use. And now this posture is extended in many different ways through the incredible work that is going on through Chris Wright and all of the Langham Partnership around the world that John set in motion.

Ornithologically Impassioned

Anyone who knows anything about John knows that the gospel in the life of John Stott would have to mention birds. Wherever he travelled, he always watched birds. John tried diligently to convert me, and many others, to birdwatching. I didn't experience a full conversion, but I did learn a lot about paying attention to the natural world, including birds, in new ways.

At one point, John was away for a couple of weeks in the Middle East. As usual, he was out doing some very early morning birdwatching when he became enthralled by a pair of beautiful rose-ringed parakeets. They are birds with bright green feathers and a very bright red band round their necks. As he followed the rose-ringed parakeets through the trees, he went through a passage without noticing that he had just entered someone's garden. He wrote in his daily journal, "I only gradually became aware that there was someone shouting in the vicinity and that I was the shoutee!" John continued, "I lowered my binoculars, and standing in front of me was an extremely angry Muslim man who was screaming at me, 'Get out! Get out of my garden!'"

John said calmly, "Do you believe in Allah?"

And the man said, "I do."

John replied, "I believe in Allah, too. I don't believe Allah would like you to be angry with me over appreciating what Allah has made." And he handed his binoculars to the man to look through. As the man handed back John's binoculars, the man said with a smile and broad gesture, "You can go anywhere in my garden!"

I love that image! I can't think of anyone else who would have had that line at that moment, not only defusing the anger, but inviting someone into such a great and wonderful celebration of God's creation.

Here, I have tried to offer some observations that are snapshots of the gospel in the life of John Stott. I hope that if you knew him, the reflections will stimulate your own memories of his life. If you did not know him, I hope you will be all the more intrigued to read what he has left behind, and to take advantage of the incredible resources of faith and life, heart and mind, that are the marks of the gospel in John Stott's life. To that end, may the gospel in all our lives bear fruit as well.

References

Brooks, David. "Who Is John Stott?" *New York Times*, 30 November 2004. https://www.nytimes.com/2004/11/30/opinion/who-is-john-stott.html.

Dudley-Smith, Timothy. *John Stott: The Making of a Leader. A Biography: The Early Years*. Downers Grove, IL: InterVarsity Press, 1999.

2

"All the Churches of Christ Greet You" (Rom 16:16)

Recognizing, Resourcing and Receiving Global Church Leaders – Celebrating the Legacy of John Stott

Chris Wright

Introduction

We might think that the world Paul had in mind when he spoke of "all the churches of Christ" (Rom 16:16) was relatively small – just the lands of the Eastern Mediterranean – even if he was writing to the church in Rome specifically to prepare them to be his sending church for his missionary intentions for Spain in the far west of the Roman Empire.

And yet, even in Paul's day, the church already had remarkable diversity – ethnic, geographical, theological and economic diversity – and was prone to division. Indeed his letter to the believers in Rome comes to its climax in his extended and impassioned appeal for mutual acceptance in chapters 14–15. "Accept/welcome one another, then," he pleads, "just as Christ accepted you, in order to bring praise to God" (Rom 15:7 NIV). This was no afterthought, just a nice polite way to end his letter; rather, for Paul, the unity of the church as a reconciled community of mutual acceptance across (especially) the Jew–Gentile barrier was a matter of utterly first importance. For how could he go and preach the gospel of reconciliation through Messiah Jesus in Spain

(Rom 15:23–32) if his sending church in Rome was a living denial of the message he proclaimed? The truth of the gospel and the credibility of his mission were both at stake.

Today we live in a global church that is vastly larger in scale than the "global" church of Paul's day. But the issues are the same in principle. It is incumbent on any part of the body of Christ to recognize and welcome others within the same global fellowship. Sadly, the church in the West (meaning predominantly the North Atlantic churches) have not been very good at doing this, partly as a result of our historical legacy of thinking of ourselves as the "home church," or the "sending church," and lumping together everywhere else as "the mission field" (even though some of the churches in Africa and Asia existed for over a thousand years before Europeans had even set foot in the Americas).

So what can we learn even from the apostle Paul's request that the churches in Rome should receive Phoebe, on Paul's commendation, as a respected church leader and patron of Christian mission, from Greece (Rom 16:1–2)? That is how he begins his long final chapter listing church leaders and apostles, Jews and Gentiles, male and female, greeting all of *them* from "all the churches of Christ," with another list of some of Paul's own companions – also markedly both Jews and Gentiles. Romans 16 is a kind of worked example (worked at considerable length!) of what he has been talking about in the previous two chapters.

At the very least we should observe the high esteem in which Paul holds so many of these named persons. He commends their hard work, their imprisonments, their life-risking courage, and how they have been tested and approved by the Lord. Would that there were such an ethos of recognition, respect and appreciation by the Western church (and theological academy) for sisters and brothers in leadership in the churches of the Global South and East.

Such an ethos was a prominent and cultivated aspect of John Stott's relationship with the global church. In his travels, he befriended church leaders from every continent, listened and learned, and took upon himself the strong commitment to do all in his power to foster their development, strengthen their resources and build their capacity.

And at the heart of John Stott's desire for his Majority World friends was that they should be men and women committed (as he himself was) to the diligent study, right handling and faithful preaching and teaching of the Word of God – with godly lives that modelled what they preached and taught. That was the foundation, he believed, on which all church leadership should be based. It is crystalized in the Vision Statement of Langham Partnership, ministries that John Stott founded nearly fifty years ago: "Our vision is to see churches in the Majority World equipped for mission and growing to maturity in Christ through the ministry of pastors and leaders who study, teach and live by the Word of God."

Below, in longer form, is John Stott's own vision. This comes from an unpublished "Personal Vision Statement" he wrote in 1996, as a way of encapsulating his rationale for the ministries, at that time, of the Langham Trust and the Evangelical Literature Trust, which are now combined within the Langham Partnership.

The Logic of John Stott's Vision

> My vision, as I look out over the world, is to see every pulpit in every church occupied by a conscientious, Bible-believing, Bible-studying, Bible-expounding pastor. I see with my mind's eye multitudes of people in every country worldwide converging on their churches every Sunday, hungry for more of God's Word. I also see pastors going to their pulpits with the Word of God in their minds (for they have studied it), in their hearts (for they have prayed over it) and on their lips (for they are intent on communicating it).
>
> What a vision! The people assemble with hunger, and preachers satisfy their hunger with God's Word! And as pastors minister to their people week after week, I see church members *changing* under the influence of God's Word, and so approximating increasingly to the kind of people God wants them to be, in understanding and obedience, in faith and love, in worship, holiness, unity, service and mission.

That last sentence is crucial. Although John Stott was one of the foremost Bible expositors of his generation, he was not interested in biblical preaching merely as an exercise in skill and performance for its own sake. He wanted church leaders and pastors to preach the Bible faithfully, so that the Bible could change the church. But he did not stop with a changed church only. The church engages in "service and mission" in the surrounding world, bearing witness to Christ as Lord of all the earth, proclaiming and demonstrating the truth of the gospel, and impacting society as salt and light in the midst of the world's corruption and darkness.

In short, John Stott wanted to see church leaders equipped to preach the Bible, so that the Bible could change the church, so that the church, in God's power, could change the world. It was a thoroughly *missional* vision (even if he did not use that particular word).

But why the emphasis on *biblical preaching*? There is, of course, more to "global church leadership" than the ability to preach the Bible well (though it is sadly one of the most neglected priorities). Once again, John Stott had his reasons. In the same unpublished statement from the 1990s he wrote,

> A new mission situation is developing in today's world, which demands a revolution in our traditional thinking. The churches of the Third World [now called the Majority World] are growing more rapidly than in the West. Many of them are more vibrant and vigorous. Already a majority of the world's Christians are non-Western and non-white.
>
> The statistics of church growth are enormously encouraging. But it is often growth without depth, and there is much superficiality *everywhere* [Stott meant in the Western church just as much as in the Majority World]. As in first-century Corinth, there is a tension between the divine ideal and the human reality, between what is and what ought to be, between the "already" and the "not yet." Thus the church is both united and divided, both holy and unholy, both the guardian of truth and prone to error. Everywhere the church boasts great things, and everywhere it fails to live up to its boasts. Its witness is marred by conspicuous failures.

Did you notice that thrice-repeated "everywhere" in John Stott's analysis? He was emphatically *not* saying that shallowness, superficiality and failure were a problem only in the Majority World. It is a problem all over the global church, including the Western church. The old derogatory saying that Christianity in Africa is "a mile wide and an inch deep" is exactly that – derogatory, both because exactly the same could be said about much Christianity in North America and my own UK, and also because some of the most profound and mature biblical and theological scholarship I know comes from Africa – as also from some parts of Asia, Latin America and the Middle East.

"Growth without depth." That was John Stott's analysis of the state of the global church. And his response, embodied in what he called "The Langham Logic" that lies behind the ministries he founded fifty years ago in 1969 and which he personally led until they consolidated into the Langham Partnership in 2001, went as follows (from my memory of him sharing it many times in public meetings):

"We have three biblical convictions," he would say, "and one inescapable conclusion":

1. God wants his church to grow up in maturity, not just to grow bigger in numbers.

2. The church grows through God's Word. Churches live, grow and flourish by the Word of God, and they languish and die without it.

3. The Word of God comes to the people of God mainly through preaching.

These three things being true, the logical question to ask is, "What can we do to raise the standards of biblical preaching?"

What John Stott had already done was to establish, in 1969 and 1971, two programmes that are now called Langham Scholars (originally the Langham Trust) and Langham Literature (originally the Evangelical Literature Trust).

The first aimed to strengthen evangelical theological education, so that future pastors who would have the benefit of seminary training (admittedly a minority) should be taught by "scholar-saints" who combine academic excellence with godly character and biblical faithfulness. So Langham Scholars funds men and women to study for PhD qualifications in biblical and theological studies, who then return to teach in seminaries in their own countries or continents.

The second, the Evangelical Literature Trust, was initially funded by Stott's decision to divert and dedicate all the financial royalties from his own writing and speaking into this Trust for the benefit of furthering Christian books in the Majority World (and his royalties still make a substantial contribution to Langham Literature's annual budget). So Stott's intention was simply to get books into the hands of pastors, students and faculty, since, as Stott said, "pastors can't preach if they don't study, and they can't study if they have no books." And of course, in the early decades of the Literature programme, that meant mostly Western books in English, French or Spanish (the colonial lingua francas) – though that has changed dramatically in the last decade.

The third Langham programme – Langham Preaching – arrived only in 2002, but it fits directly into Stott's vision and is resourced massively from the other two older programmes. It facilitates movements for training in biblical preaching, serving thousands of pastors and lay preachers in every continent.

There are of course other agencies with similar goals to Langham Partnership, with whom we enjoy godly fellowship and cooperation. But as we celebrate John Stott's vision and legacy here, I share with you primarily about Langham, as a "case study" of one major dimension of how God used his life and commitments for the strengthening of the global church.

I have three questions in relation to the strengthening of global church leadership: What? How? and Why? What has been accomplished? How has it impacted? and Why does it matter? We will address each question in turn.

What Has Been Accomplished through John Stott's Vision?

From their humble beginnings some fifty years ago, the ministries that John Stott initiated have expanded and borne fruit in amazing ways, under God's blessing and empowering. I hope you can bear some statistics, remembering that for every number or percentage many stories could be told, names named and places visited all over the world. And these findings are not "guesstimates," but the verified result of independent surveys of all three programmes that have been going on since 2015, conducted by the measurement and evaluation work of the philanthropic advisory agency "Excellence in Giving."[1] The statistics that follow were the reported outcomes and impacts for Langham financial year up to the end of June 2019.

The Langham Scholars Programme

The aim of this programme is to enhance evangelical theological education in the Majority World by enabling academically able and spiritually committed men and women to gain their doctorates in biblical and theological studies and return to teach in their own countries or continents.

- In the past 40 years, more than 300 Scholars from 71 nations have been funded to this level, and just over 90% of those selected and who successfully completed during that period have fulfilled their commitment to return home.
- In the past academic year, Langham supported 73 students from 41 countries who are pursuing their doctoral studies, with 18 having commenced last year.
- Whereas originally candidates studied in British universities and then in seminaries in the USA and Canada, Langham has been instrumental in facilitating the development of high-quality doctoral

---

1. Excellence in Giving, https://www.excellenceingiving.com/.

programmes in some fine theological institutions in the Majority World. So now about 56% of our current doctoral candidates are studying for their doctorates in South Africa, Nigeria, India, the Philippines and continental Europe, as well as Australia, New Zealand and Hong Kong.

- A survey of 149 graduated Scholars in 2017 found that
  - 80% were teaching students who had gone on to start new ministries, plant churches and related activities;
  - 78% had expanded the scope of theological education in their countries by adding new degree courses, gaining accreditation, expanding student intake and similar initiatives;
  - 42% had written the first ever book in their own national language on the study of the Bible, or on issues in theology and mission;
  - 34% had received on average two offers of jobs in the West (the attraction and temptation can be enormous), but only 5% of those surveyed are currently working in Western countries – showing a very high commitment to the aims and values of the programme.

The Langham Literature Programme

The Langham Literature programme has several arms. We distribute books in multiple languages, but we also strive to foster indigenous evangelical writers, editors and publishers to multiply contextually relevant books for their own people. And as Langham, we publish predominantly Majority World (MW) authored books, making them both affordable and accessible (in print and digital platforms) – giving a voice to those who otherwise are never heard. Again, a few verified facts and statistics from June 2019:

- In the past year alone, Langham distributed just over 53,000 books to Majority World readers. About 30% of these went to 773 Majority World seminaries in 84 countries, through the library grant programme. The rest went to pastors, students, ministry partners, and participants in Langham Preaching movements.
- We supported 22 indigenous evangelical publishing houses in 20 Majority World countries, enabling them to publish 47 more titles in local languages.

- We continued the training of 11 Majority World editors and 14 Majority World writers.
- We published 47 books under our various imprints, 31 being by Majority World authors, including 10 Langham Scholars.
- We completed the publication of three large one-volume regional commentaries on the whole Bible entirely written by biblical scholars indigenous to their own region: the Hausa translation of the *Africa Bible Commentary*; the *Arabic Bible Commentary*; the *Latin American Bible Commentary*. These now join the already published *South Asia Bible Commentary* and the *Slavic Bible Commentary* (Russian and Ukrainian).
- Based on a survey of 310 seminaries in 67 countries between 2015 and 2017,
  - 27% of them had added 3 new courses per year as a direct result of receiving books and library support from Langham;
  - 40% of them had obtained accreditation because of Langham's investment in enhancing their libraries;
  - 17% of them switched course textbooks from Western to non-Western culturally relevant books, facilitated through Langham writers and publishing support.

The Langham Preaching Programme

Langham Preaching aims to establish indigenous movements that champion faithful biblical preaching. This is accomplished through a combination of week-long training seminars for pastors and preachers in their own countries; building networks of very local "preachers' clubs" – groups that meet usually monthly for mutual encouragement, training and learning; training local and national facilitators; and entrusting national, regional and continental oversight to indigenous leaders under an international leadership team.

As of June 2019,

- Langham Preaching has held 338 preaching training seminars in 70 preaching movements all over the world. In any given week, there will be several Langham Preaching seminars at different levels taking place somewhere around the world.
- It is estimated (this is an estimate!) that more than 10,000 pastors will be impacted by this training each year.

- We have continued the training of 545 local facilitators who are engaged in training others.
- We have supported 1,190 preachers' clubs (of 7–10 pastors normally), who meet regularly.

A survey of those who had participated in 178 Preaching movements in 24 nations over three years showed that more than half of them now were preaching through whole books of the Bible one passage at a time, their sermon preparation time had more than doubled, and the proportion of those who said that previously they just preached with no preparation had dropped from a quarter to less than 5 percent.

So then, across a wide range of inputs and outputs, God has been using the vision he first entrusted to John Stott to strengthen the leadership of the global church primarily through equipping and resourcing those who serve the church in teaching and preaching the Word of God.

How Were John Stott and the Global Church Mutually Impacted?

John Stott was a quintessential Englishman! He readily acknowledged the blessings and privileges of his family background (son of a knighted and decorated medical practitioner in London), his education (Rugby School and Cambridge University) and the influence and shaping of his life by the historically strong British evangelical heritage, writings and traditions. But he also had a profoundly Christlike humility, a love for people and a willingness to listen and learn. In his extensive travels in the continents of the Global South, he built deep and respectful friendships with church leaders, young and old, in those regions.

And he was greatly disturbed and pained, not only by the shallowness of the church everywhere ("growth without depth") that I mentioned above, but also by the gross imbalance that he witnessed. On the one hand, there is the church in the West that is rich in material wealth and the theological resources of centuries of Christian scholarship and books. On the other hand, there are the churches in the Global South. Some of them (such as Ethiopia, India and Palestine) are more ancient than the Western church. Many of them are relatively young in church and mission history. Most of them struggle with debilitating poverty, lack of resources (material and theological) and the pressures of persecution and conflicts – and yet they are often vibrant, joyful and growing, or, at least, growing numerically if not in depth, as he observed.

John responded with a characteristic blend of humility and compassion. Basically, he simply wanted to help sisters and brothers in need – entirely in the spirit of Christ and the apostles. However, his vision was informed by much more than compassion and generosity alone, in two respects at least.

First, John Stott utterly repudiated any kind of paternalism. He did not think in terms of "us mature and wealthy Christians in the West" stooping down to help "you immature and needy Christians in the rest of the world." Nor did he think in mere "management-speak" or with superhero arrogance: "They've got a big problem; we've got the perfect solution." Rather, he had a very real and sincere respect for the wide network of friends he had made among the church leaders in Africa, Latin America, Asia, the Middle East, Eastern Europe and elsewhere. He treated them as spiritual equals, with love and dignity. And they knew it, and reciprocated with their own love for him. So, to quote again from that Vision Statement of the 1990s (already decades after his ministries had been launched), "The question is what we in the West may be able to contribute, *with a love that is genuinely fraternal and free of paternalism*, to the continuing growth into Christian maturity of the burgeoning churches of the Majority World."

So he asked questions, listened carefully to the answers, and sought to align his own vision and ministry initiatives with the expressed visions and desires of those he sought to serve. He did not impose a Western-framed and -franchised product on Majority World churches. He did not build institutions or organizations in his own name. (He named the original Langham Trust after the street in London where his church was situated – All Souls Church, Langham Place – and he famously did not like it when the Langham Foundation in the USA changed its name to John Stott Ministries, requesting shortly before his death that they remove his name and return to the Langham identity – which they gladly did.) He did not insist on his own agenda or preferred models. He came alongside Majority World churches and leaders and responded to what they said they most needed. And that has remained an essential element of the Langham DNA ever since.

Second, and as the major reason for the impact his vision has had (to come at last to answering the question posed above), John Stott believed strongly in *mutuality and reciprocity* within the global church. Though a son of the Western church, John Stott, like the apostle Paul, was passionately committed to the worldwide body of Christ. He not only knew and loved so many church leaders in many denominations outside the West and far beyond his own beloved Anglican Communion, he also wanted to enable their voices to be heard, to affirm their leadership, to facilitate the development of their giftings, academically and spiritually. "We must be global Christians," he used to say, "with a global vision, because our God is a global God."

I have sometimes said that John Stott was both apostolic and Abrahamic. There was something *apostolic* about his evangelistic commitment to the gospel and to the faithful teaching of biblical truth. And there was something *Abrahamic* about his "all nations" perspective. Not only was he himself a blessing to many nations, he also modelled and taught the "obedience of faith" (to quote Paul) that characterized Abraham's combination of faith demonstrated in works (to quote James, e.g. Jas 2:20–26). So, for John Stott, to strengthen the leadership of the church *outside* the West would be to strengthen *global* church leadership, *including* the West. He prayed and longed for the greater health and maturity of the worldwide church, including the West. So whatever he could do to strengthen the Majority World church, the whole body of Christ would benefit.

Stott recognized an additional benefit that would adorn the truth of the gospel. As the leadership of the global church outside the West was strengthened, resourced and recognized, then the truly international, multicultural nature of the church itself would be far more visible and more in line with the biblical portrait of the church. And this would be so much more attractive as a showcase for the biblical gospel than a church so overwhelmingly dominated by the history and cultures of the Western church, with its mixture of successful but stalled growth, profound but limited theological scholarship, legacies of Christendom and colonialism, cultural syncretism and idolatry, superiority tendencies, and un-Christlike obsession with power and questionable wealth.

Indeed, one can go further than simply pointing out that the church in the West stands to *benefit* from the strengthening and maturing of church leadership outside the West. To be blunt, it may be a matter not merely of benefit but of survival. After all, where is the church growing, in numbers, maturity, theology, mission and societal influence? Largely in the continents of the South. And where is the church shrinking? Largely in the West – with some exceptions, of course, but in broad terms the Western church is either static or shrinking in multiple ways. To quote from the Eerdmans blog (introducing their Majority World Theology series):

> The church has moved. The North Atlantic region was once the unrivaled center of the Christian faith. But the gospel has run throughout the world, and the new centers of Christianity are found in the global South and East, places that many of us call the Majority World. Cities like Seoul, Nairobi, and São Paulo are now

the urban powerhouses of the Christian faith. Christians in the [W]est are discovering that they are on the demographic margins of the church. The shift in the population center of Christianity has implications for biblical studies and theology.[2]

We who are Western Christians need help. We need to acknowledge that we are the minority church in global terms. We need to recognize the vast and alarming extent to which, like the people of Israel before the exile, we have succumbed to a range of idolatries and syncretisms – "going after the gods of the people around us" (to paraphrase the frequent warnings of Deuteronomy). We should be lamenting the way many who profess to be Christian succumb to frightening collusion with political leaders and policies that bear no resemblance whatsoever to the teachings and demands of Christ.

We ask, with the psalmist, "Where shall our help come from?" (cf. Ps 121:1).

Well, from God of course, we desperately pray. But what has God been doing this past half century and more? The same as he has done throughout the centuries of church history. As one centre of mature and missional Christian presence falls into decline, God raises up another elsewhere. What, then, will it mean that the Christian church has been growing so remarkably in other parts of the world, including in countries that in sheer numerical terms are bound to become major global powers in the present century – China and India?

It is from these regions of Asia, and from Africa and Latin America, that God is already raising up leaders, scholars, thinkers, writers and preachers who can speak with the authenticity of their contexts (and especially the authenticity of suffering for the Word of God and the testimony of Jesus Christ) into the moribund churches of the West. And some of those emerging (and already fully emerged and established) leaders are undoubtedly part of the fruit of John Stott's vision and initiatives. As Tim Keller has said in commending Langham's work, "John Stott foresaw the rise of Christianity in the Global South before most anybody. He got there and saw the need for training. . . . This ministry has been a game changer."

So there is, in my view, a rather delightful irony about how John Stott's vision has turned out. His initiatives for theological education and literature were initially born of his desire that the well-resourced Western church should come alongside the under-resourced churches of the Global South with generous assistance. But in God's long-term providence and the grand sweep of church history, there will most likely be a reverse impact. Stott's efforts

---

2. Green, "Meet These Books."

will have helped to empower and equip the non-Western churches to come to the aid of the Western church in its decline. We in the West are already finding ourselves the recipients and beneficiaries of the spiritual, missional and theological leadership in the non-Western church that is in part the fruit of such investment over decades.

John Stott, who set out to help the Majority World church to mature, may end up having helped the Western church to survive.

I think that makes God smile. It sure makes me smile!

This symposium collection itself is part of that smile. Several of our main contributors are Langham Scholars, who are not only in significant leadership roles in their own contexts, but who are heard and rightly respected in the Western church (when it is prepared to listen).

- I see this "reverse" impact of Stott's "investment" that I have suggested above when I listen to an Indian woman Scholar, Dr Havilah Dharamraj, give main-stage and greatly appreciated Bible teaching in July 2019 at the oldest prestigious Bible convention in Britain – the Keswick Convention.
- I see it in the increasing number of Langham Scholars who are being invited to participate and contribute in flagship events of the Western theological academy, such as the Evangelical Theological Society, Society for Biblical Literature, Tyndale Fellowship Study Groups, and other forums.
- I see it in the participation of two Indian Langham Scholars, with PhDs in Old and New Testament, on the Committee for Bible Translation of the NIV.
- I see it in the willingness of a Western publisher like Zondervan to publish with North American rights Langham-sponsored one-volume commentaries on the whole Bible entirely written by Majority World scholars, such as the *Africa Bible Commentary* and the *South Asian Bible Commentary*.
- I see it in the number of Majority World colleagues who are now exercising senior leadership in global organizations and agencies, such as IFES, SU, Lausanne, WEA and INFEMIT, and also in mission agencies that have been traditionally Western in membership and leadership, such as the Baptist Missionary Society, the Church Mission Society, SIM, and others.
- I see it in the initiative of Wheaton College's own Gene Green (recently retired), along with K. K. Yeo and Stephen Pardue, to

generate the Majority World Theology Series, published by Eerdmans and hosting conferences at SBL each year, with volumes such as *Jesus Without Borders: Christology in the Majority World*; *The Spirit over the Earth: Pneumatology in the Majority World*; and *The Trinity among the Nations: The Doctrine of God in the Majority World*. Gene, who profoundly shared John Stott's vision and served for years on the board of Langham Partnership USA, strongly advocating for our Langham Scholar programme, has been outstanding in his commitment to Majority World and Native American theology and training.

- I see it in the increasing volume of theological books by Majority World authors that are being made available in the West. Have you seen the Langham Monograph Series – some fifty titles now of Majority World PhD dissertations on a massive range of biblical, theological, missiological and contextual topics? Or the Langham Global Library, with more than thirty titles predominantly by Majority World authors and all of global interest and relevance?

But the question is: Are we listening? It's not just a question of being humble enough as Western Christians to consider that we might have something to learn (a lot to learn!) from our sisters and brothers who constitute the largest and growing part of God's church on earth. It's also being informed enough to know they even exist and have something to say! Sadly, so many Western churches and seminaries remain encased in the bubble (to mix metaphors rather alarmingly) of Western ecclesiology, history and theological writing. To quote again from the *EerdWord* blog:

> The question that remains is "What's on your bookshelf?" Which authors do we assign to our students? Whom do we pick up to read? Some years ago the Kenyan New Testament scholar John Mbiti said this to Western Christians: "We have eaten theology with you; we have drunk theology with you; we have dreamed theology with you. But it has been all one-sided; it has all been, in a sense, your theology. . . . We know you theologically. The question is, 'Do you know us theologically? Would you like to know us theologically? Can you know us theologically?' . . . You have become a major subconscious part of our theologizing, and we are privileged to be so involved in you through the fellowship we

share in Christ. When will you make us part of your subconscious process of theologizing?"[3]

It would be a much more tragic irony, it seems to me, if, having played his part in strengthening the leadership of the global church, John Stott departed this life with the Western church still failing to be blessed and benefited by what God is so excitingly doing elsewhere in the world.

Why Does It Matter?

Finally, and briefly, why does it matter that John Stott and Langham Partnership emphasize so much the importance of strengthening global church leadership especially in the realm of theological education and the faithful teaching and preaching of the Bible? One answer comes from the Cape Town Commitment:

> The mission of the Church on earth is to serve the mission of God, and the mission of theological education is to strengthen and accompany the mission of the Church. Theological education serves *first* to train those who lead the Church as pastor-teachers, equipping them to teach the truth of God's Word with faithfulness, relevance and clarity; and *second*, to equip all God's people for the missional task of understanding and relevantly communicating God's truth in every cultural context. Theological education engages in spiritual warfare, as "we demolish arguments and every pretension that sets itself up against the knowledge of God, and we take captive every thought to make it obedient to Christ" [2 Cor 10:4–5].
>
> Those of us who lead churches and mission agencies need to acknowledge that theological education is *intrinsically* missional. Those of us who provide theological education need to ensure that it is *intentionally* missional, since its place within the academy is not an end in itself, but to serve the mission of the Church in the world.[4]

Theological education, on this understanding, is one dimension of the church's mandate to teach. Teaching is integral to the Great Commission and one of the gifts of the Spirit. And teachers are among the gifts of the ascended Christ to his church. So teaching should be happening throughout the church's life

---

3. Green.

4. Lausanne Movement, "Cape Town Commitment," II.F.4.

and ministry – not just in the formal seminary training of future pastors for ordained ministry.[5]

However, the simplest answer to our question "Why does such faithful teaching matter?" is: because the Bible commands it and the church needs it.

The Bible affirms from very early on, and repeatedly in both Testaments, that God's people need teaching and teachers, and that God's people are vulnerable and endangered when teachers are either absent, or false and unfaithful.

- God mandated *Abraham* to teach his household and descendants the way of the Lord, by doing righteousness and justice – in the context of God's promise and calling that Israel would become a blessing to all nations. There is a *missional* dimension here: if God's people are to bear witness among the nations to the living God, then they need to be taught to walk in his ways (Gen 18:18–19).
- God mandated *Moses* to teach the Israelites, and Moses mandated Israel's parents and priests to be teachers of God's word to their people – in the context of surrounding plurality of gods and idols. There is a *monotheistic* dimension here: if God's people are to remain faithful to the one true living God, they need to pay constant heed to his teaching (Deut 4 and 6).
- *Paul* mandated Timothy and Titus to follow his own example as diligent and hardworking teachers of the Scriptures – in the context of the threatening falsehoods both outside and within the church. There is a *maturity* dimension here, since Paul urges such teaching so that believers might grow up in their knowledge of the faith and their living of it with endurance and joy (Eph 4:11–13; Col 1:9–11).

To summarize, God has ordained that there should be teachers and teaching within the people of God:

- so that God's people as a whole might be a community fit for participation in *God's own mission* to bring blessing to the nations (the Abrahamic goal);
- so that God's people as a whole might remain committed to *the one true God* revealed in the Bible (as YHWH in Old Testament Israel,

---

5. A more extended version of the summarized reflections of this final section can be found in my chapter "The Missional Nature and Role of Theological Education," in Dirk R. Buursma, Katya Covrett and Verlyn D. Verbrugge (eds.), *Evangelical Scholarship, Retrospects and Prospects: Essays in Honor of Stanley N. Gundry* (Grand Rapids, MI: Zondervan, 2017), 225–254.

and incarnate in Jesus of Nazareth in the New Testament), and resist all the surrounding idolatries of their cultures (the Mosaic goal); and

- so that God's people as a whole might *grow to maturity* in the understanding, the obedience and the endurance of faith, and in effective mission in the world (the Pauline goal).

So here is the question to be faced by every institution of Christian education in the global church: Are we aiming to produce women and men who, in whatever vocation they have from God in the church and the world, are *biblically mission-minded*, *biblically monotheistic* and *biblically mature*?

I think John Stott would have agreed with those objectives, and we can celebrate the fact that those characteristics are very visibly present in so many of those whom his ministries have nurtured, resourced and encouraged into their current roles in global church leadership.

References

Green, Gene L. "Meet These Books: Majority World Theology Series." *Eerdword* (blog), 10 November 2017. https://eerdword.com/2017/11/10/meet-these-books-majority-world-theology-series/.

Lausanne Movement. "The Cape Town Commitment." 2011. https://www.lausanne.org/content/ctcommitment#capetown.

Stott, John R. W. "Personal Vision Statement." 1996. Unpublished.

Part 2

Christian Social
Engagement

3

The Image of God and Justice

Myrto Theocharous

Introduction

John Stott, in his book *Issues Facing Christians Today*, wrote a brief history of justice violations in the modern world and traced the history of the idea of human rights in the West and beyond. Stott's concern was that there is more discussion about what human *rights* are than about what a *human* is. Cultures, he says, have rushed to decide what human dignity looks like, and imposed that idea on other traditions where human dignity may look completely different. For Stott, what is of primary importance is understanding what it is to be human and what human responsibility – more so than rights – is.[1] This shift of emphasis comes close to the purpose of this chapter concerning what the image of God is.

In Christian discussions about human rights, the language of image is usually evoked in order to justify *why* a person is entitled to these rights. If a person is in the image of God, then he or she is the rightful *recipient* of all forms of justice. This use of "image" language with a focus on the recipient of justice is thus limited to discussions of human rights – not animal rights, for example. What is it, then, that makes an *animal* the rightful recipient of justice? The fact that we cannot speak of the image of God in the animal is perhaps an indicator that "image" language should primarily be a descriptor of the giver rather than of the recipient of justice.

In this chapter I will argue that the language of image should be used primarily for the *doers* or *givers* of justice and secondarily for the *recipients* of

---

1. Stott, *Issues Facing Christians Today*, 189–213.

justice.[2] From my own experience with victims of sex trafficking, whenever I used to look at the degraded bodies of abused women in the brothels, I would remind myself that these oppressed human beings were God's images and, therefore, deserving of our justice. Or, whenever I encountered inhumane conditions in the camps in which refugees were placed, my whole being would object to such treatment because these refugees were God's images, and therefore deserving of our justice. This is a perfectly legitimate way of thinking, but I realized that this kind of language betrayed that what was being questioned or was "at stake" was the image of God in the recipient of justice, while the image of God in the church, in the activist, in the potential giver of justice, was taken as a given. I found myself trying to argue for affirming, proving or establishing that those in need are in the image of God in order to motivate into action Christians in whom the image of God was taken as firmly established (whether they were moved to action or not).

I have come to realize that this should be reversed. The image of God in the recipient is never up for debate in the Old Testament. It is assumed. God is always identified with the oppressed. Instead, the real question is the following: Can a Christian who refuses justice to another, whether a human or a non-human recipient, be called "the image of God"?

By examining the expression "image of God" in its Old Testament context, as well as in its ancient Near Eastern context, my purpose is not to overthrow centuries of theological reflection on the image of God. I shall merely attempt to shift the emphasis of the image discourse on to the givers rather than the recipients of justice, in the hope that some insights may be helpful in enriching our understanding of our identity and role as Christians.

The Image of God as a Royal Role

Versions of the expression that humans have been created "according to the image and likeness of God" are encountered only three times in the Old Testament, and all of these are found in the beginning chapters of the book of Genesis.[3]

Here I will focus more on the *royal* function of image. Biblical scholarship has, more or less, reached a consensus that the expression "according to the

---

2. The expression "image of God" that we have in Jas 3:9 is used for the recipient rather than the agent. This is a valid use of the expression but it should not overshadow the dominant use of the expression in the OT that applies to the doer of justice.

3. Gen 1:26–27 (*tselem, demut; tselem*); 5:1, 3 (*demut; demut, tselem*); 9:6 (*tselem*).

image" denotes a *royal role*. This conclusion is reached not only from the first chapter of Genesis, but also from the use of the expression in Egyptian and Mesopotamian texts. The royal aspect has not been sufficiently explored in theology, so I hope to see more theological reflection on it in future.[4] As I shall demonstrate in this chapter, I believe that the royal understanding of the image is absolutely crucial for the church to grasp and take on for its identity and social presence today.

Regardless of the fact that the expressions "image" and "likeness" have served as fertile ground for the endless pursuit, in the patristic writings and beyond, of what a human in the image of God is, in the biblical text the emphasis is on the *function* of the image bearer: not on what an image bearer *is*, but on what an image bearer *does*.

The royal role of God's image is communicated through the word "dominion," used twice in Genesis 1:26–28, over non-human creation.[5] Dominion is that aspect of image that Psalm 8 also understands as central, thus confirming the royal function of humanity: "You have given them *dominion* over the works of your hands; you have put all things under their feet" (Ps 8:6; emphasis added).

This, of course, has nothing to do with the abuse of creation in the modern world. The verbs *radah*, "to have dominion" (Gen 1:26, 28), and *mashal*, "to rule or govern" (Ps 8:6), are common and refer even to the simple act of cultivating the ground (Gen 2:15) or taming animals – in other words, the minimum requirements for the organization of basic human society.[6]

In ancient Egypt, the king was called the image of the god Re, of Ammon-Re, of Horus, of Attum and of Ammon, and the central role of the king, as an embodiment of the deity (in the same way one of the deity's statues would be

---

4. Holsclaw, "Reviewing David Bentley Hart." David Bentley Hart has been recently criticized for neglecting this aspect of *imago Dei* in his book *That All Shall Be Saved* and limiting himself to the ontological understanding. This may be a major factor determining his conclusions about the inescapability of universalism. See the review by Geoff Holsclaw cited at Patheos, 2 October 19, https://www.patheos.com/blogs/jesuscreed/2019/10/02/reviewing-david-bentley-hart/?fbclid=IwAR0OapxeMOSTectm4xe5s7dw3D9dWxC9c371KPsQpiZklGxPrKNI6JGlnvs.

5. "Then God said, 'Let us make humankind in our image, according to our likeness; and let them have *dominion* over the fish of the sea, and over the birds of the air, and over the cattle, and over all the wild animals of the earth, and over every creeping thing that creeps upon the earth. . . . Be fruitful and multiply, and fill the earth and subdue it; and have *dominion* over the fish of the sea and over the birds of the air and over every living thing that moves upon the earth'" (Gen 1:26–28; emphasis added).

6. Gordon, *Genesis 1–11*, 10; Middleton, *Liberating Image*, 60. *Radah* is used to emphasize humane ways of ruling in Lev 25:43 and Ezek 34:4; Blenkinsopp, *Creation, De-Creation, Re-Creation*, 26. For contemporary political dangers of the royal model, see Middleton, 35.

considered), was mediatory. He was the one who would bridge the two spheres, heaven and earth. For example, Amon-Re says about Amenotep III: "You are my beloved son, the one who came from my loins, my image, which I have placed on this earth. I assigned to you the governance of the land with peace."[7]

In Mesopotamia, just as in Egypt, only the *king* was called "the image of God." Practically, this meant that the king was obliged to listen to his people, pay attention to their issues and offer his counsel. It also meant that his word had authority.[8] The king, as well as the god whom he represented, executed right judgment in the affairs of the people, but also displayed acts of mercy towards them.[9]

In describing the creation of Adam, then, the author, having in mind the ancient Near Eastern understanding of the king as the image of God, is using this exact same expression, applying it provocatively to humanity at large. This radical democratization of the expression "image of God" overturns the default royal ideology of the ancient world. It amounts to an ideological revolution, if you will, against the oppressive centres of power of the Egyptian rule over Canaan or against later imperial powers, depending on the date each scholar would give to these texts. According to Eckart Otto, these polemic texts were formulated against the Assyrian and Babylonian cosmogony and anthropology that these empires presupposed in forming their royal ideologies.[10]

At the same time, these texts oppose the royal ideology of Israel as well.[11] As Middleton proposes, this is not a critique of the type "us against them," God's people versus the pagans, but primarily an internal critique of Israel's mimesis of imperial models.[12] Imperial ideology has seeped into the people of God, into the church, who are not thinking very differently from the way their neighbours think.

---

7. Blenkinsopp, 109–111. In the teaching of Merikare, an older Egyptian text, there is the idea that humans are the images of God who came out of his body. This idea is not about democratization because the idea precedes the royal understanding of image. Even though this idea could have developed into something analogous to the democratized view of the image that is found in Genesis, it seems to have been silenced. On the contrary, the king as the image of God was the prevalent understanding that dominated in the Egyptian literature (Blenkinsopp, 100–104).

8. Blenkinsopp, 111–113.

9. Blenkinsopp, 113.

10. Otto, "Human Rights."

11. Otto, 12. This is particularly against the elite class of the southern kingdom of Judah, which is eventually defeated in 587 BC.

12. Middleton, *Liberating Image*, 195.

In other words, if the king as the "image of God" means that he rules and effects justice on earth just as his god would do, then for Genesis *every* human has that authority, and *every* human is a carrier of justice on earth. However, in Genesis 1, this idea is expressed as authority of humans over non-human creation, namely a responsibility for the flourishing of non-human creation, just as God had already demonstrated in Genesis 1:30 ("[to] everything that has the breath of life, I have given every green plant for food"). It is only when we arrive at Genesis 9 that we see the role of the image of God in human society *after* the fall, where, paradoxically, the role of humanity as the image of God is not withdrawn (Gen 5:3).

The Image of God in a Fallen World

We are no longer in the dreamy world of the garden of Eden, but in a world where the murder of innocent Abel (Gen 4), the mass rape of women (Gen 6) and the uncontrollable shedding of blood that brought about the flood (Gen 6:11–12)[13] have followed. How should a human act as an image of God in this new context of violence – *our* world's context of violence?

In Genesis 9:6 we have the third and final mention of the human being as the image of God. The text reads as follows:

> Whoever sheds the blood of a human,
> By a human shall his blood be shed,
> For according to the image of God he's made the human.[14]

This is a passage that is very hard to swallow in our contemporary world with the sensitivities of our age regarding capital punishment. As violent as it may appear, it is worth attempting to understand it since it is so intricately connected to what it means for a person to be the image of God in a fallen world.

This text should not be interpreted in the classic way. Its meaning is not that the person who is *murdered* is in God's image and, therefore, retribution should be made against the murderer. What the text is actually saying, according to everything we have seen with respect to the image of God consisting of a royal role of authority, is that the person who is expected to effect justice for the sake of the victim is authorized to do so precisely because he or she is acting as the image of God. In other words, the family of the victim does not have to wait

---

13. For the meaning of the word *hamas* see Frymer-Kensky, "Atrahasis Epic," 153.

14. My translation. For an understanding of the different prepositions in the text, see Zehnder, "Cause or Value?," 81–89.

for God to come down and bring retribution for the crime, even though there are numerous prayers that beg God for such vengeance;[15] such prayers rather reveal the failure of the justice system. Instead, the family of the victim can expect justice from fellow humans who are effecting justice on behalf of God. This text tells us that a human being, because he or she is the image of God, is authorized to avenge the blood of the victim him- or herself.[16] Therefore, the verse says that by a human being the blood of the murderer will be shed because, as an image of God, a human being is authorized to do so.

A multitude of texts present God as the one who avenges the blood of the innocent (e.g. Ps 9:12: "For he who avenges blood is mindful of them; he does not forget the cry of the afflicted").[17] Similarly, kings, as the deity's representative, the deity's image, had the role of carrying out retributive justice for innocent blood that had been shed. The power to put a person to death is related to Pharaoh (Gen 40:19, 22; Exod 2:15; 10:28), King Saul (1 Sam 11:13 MT), King David (2 Sam 11:15; 21:6), Joash (2 Chr 24:21), Jehoiakim (Jer 26:21) and King Darius (Ezra 6:11).[18] Avenging innocent blood was considered the prerogative of the king who acted in imitation of the deity.

But this absolute authority over life and death was meant to serve justice, the cause of the innocent, not the royal interests. Psalm 72, for example, tells us that the ideal king is the one who gives justice to the poor and frees the weak who beg for help; verse 14 says:

> From oppression and violence he redeems their life;
> and precious is their blood in his sight.

Being an image of God meant being the person to whom the oppressed might run to find justice. Kings were meant to serve this function, but let us not forget that in the history of Israel, the king was very often the perpetrator, the one who shed innocent blood, and God often raised up lay Israelites for the task of defending blood (e.g. Ahab and Jezebel, 2 Kgs 9:7; Hos 1:4; Jeremiah

---

15. E.g. Pss 7:8; 26:1; 43:1.

16. This particular reading of the verse has also been proposed by Wilson, "Blood Vengeance," 263–273. Wilson refers to three more scholars who share this same view: Berndt J. Diebner, H. Schult and Jeffrey H. Tigay (268 n. 18).

17. See also Pss 55:23; 59:2; 139:19.

18. Texts such as Eccl 8:2–4, which says that it is important to act properly before a king lest you are punished, presuppose this royal power to effectively execute judgment (cf. also Prov 16:15).

warned the king of Judah to stop shedding innocent blood, Jer 22:3, 15–16; Nebuchadnezzar killed whomever he willed, Dan 5:19).[19]

Of course, there is always a reason why governments kill. The shedding of blood in the great empires, such as the Assyrian Empire, was justified for the sake of the preservation of order, security and justice. Often it was done simply in order to inspire fear.[20] In many Assyrian texts it is apparent that the king was identified with the notion of order and justice to such an extent that any kind of criticism against him was regarded as treason, a betrayal of this order that his empire strived to secure. The government had to be protected at all costs because even the slightest questioning of the empire could open the doors to chaos and instability. Therefore, any critique of the empire was equal to revolt against the only representative of God on earth, and consequently against God himself.[21] In Genesis 9:6, God appears to remove the exclusivity of the divine role of blood avenger from the king and to hand it over to every human, since every human is God's image.

At this point we need to let the magnitude of this task we have been given sink in and to reflect on what a weighty statement it is to claim that "I am God's image." It should be a terrifying notion for a person to make such a declaration.

A simplistic understanding of Genesis 9:6 that disregards its canonical impact would hastily conclude that being the image of God means that I can effect capital punishment. But it is not that simple. The biblical texts already sense the danger of abusing capital punishment.[22] What happens if there is a mistake and an innocent person is punished instead of the guilty one? What happens if someone accuses a person of murder without any evidence? What happens if it was just an accident and the death was not premeditated? What if the killing was the result of self-defence? Is there, perhaps, a punishment

---

19. The great emperors would shed the blood of the people, and texts such as the following authorized the people to act as God's images by bringing about justice themselves: "Will not your own creditors suddenly rise, and those who make you tremble wake up? Then you will be booty for them. Because you have plundered many nations, all that survive of the peoples shall plunder you – because of human bloodshed, and violence to the earth, to cities and all who live in them. . . . Alas for you who build a town by bloodshed, and found a city on iniquity! . . . For the violence done to Lebanon will overwhelm you; the destruction of the animals will terrify you – because of human bloodshed and violence to the earth, to cities and all who live in them" (Hab 2:7–8, 12, 17).

20. See Dickson, "Kingship as Racketeering," 311–328.

21. Otto, "Human Rights," 8–9.

22. Already we see in the LXX translation of Gen 9:6 that "by a human" has been removed, possibly creating an understanding in this way that such a serious task is nobody's prerogative. This kind of anxiety is confirmed in the handling of the death penalty in the rabbinic sources and in the textual intrusions of the targumists. See Priest, "Gen 9:6," 145–151.

equal to the death penalty that could be applied so that we may leave the final word to God himself?

As the rest of the Scriptures will show, it is not upholding the particular *type* of punishment that makes one the image of God. The punishment is beside the point. The development of Israelite law will show that being God's image means having a deeper concern about proper trial procedures with the purpose of limiting the power of prominent individuals, such as male heads of households, over weaker members of society. It is about preventing powerful individuals from taking the law into their own hands.[23]

The worries that we mentioned about procedures are worries that are already present in the texts and they are not any different from arguments that we propose today against capital punishment. A dialectic on what is just is initiated in the Old Testament itself, and we are heirs of this ability to reflect and to negotiate justice today, not just for capital crimes but for all issues, rather than receiving a verdict straight from the mouth of a king. Genesis 9:6 places God's people on a trajectory of figuring out when justice is served and when it is not. And if capital punishment, the most extreme case of justice, demands such wisdom and reflection, then that is indicative of what is expected of humans towards *all* matters of justice.

This divine task of justice, this responsibility for the lives of others, was not taken lightly. God's people have been seeking ways of handling the difficult and sacred task of justice with much "fear and trembling," lest they themselves become unjust. Examples include the first act of God's people in the land of Canaan. They appointed cities of refuge which would function as asylums for the perpetrator (local or foreign) so that his or her life might be safe until all the legal processes had been carried out.[24] Legislation for determining the guilty party in a crime was becoming more and more strict, taking into consideration the location of the perpetrator, the weapon that was used[25] and whether the person acted out of self-defence;[26] the requirement for at least two or three witnesses for an accusation to stand was also added.[27]

---

23. See Holtz, "Stoning the Idolater."

24. Exod 21:13; Num 35:11, 15; Deut 4:41; 19:2, 4–6; Josh 20:9.

25. Num 35:20–21, 16–18.

26. Exod 22:2–3.

27. Deut 17:6; 19:15. These are elements supported in the Universal Declaration of Human Rights, articles 10 and 11: https://www.un.org/en/universal-declaration-human-rights/. Israelite society developed and moved to a period where the head of the family was not the absolute legal authority – i.e. a father could not put his own child to death: judgment would go through the legal processes of the elders of the town (Deut 21:18–21). See de Vaux, *Ancient Israel*, 23.

Finally, texts betray the possible replacement of capital punishment with exile.[28] This alternative may have been inspired by the way in which God himself, a few chapters before Genesis 9, handled the murderer Cain. According to the law, capital punishment should have been imposed for the innocent blood of Abel. Instead of this, God exiles Cain (4:12), providing some sort of asylum that forbids his killing,[29] thus problematizing the handling of capital punishment for the readers of the story.[30] Even the exile of Israel itself is often presented in the prophetic texts as the appropriate punishment for the shedding of blood in their land, instead of the total annihilation of the people.[31]

Moreover, by preaching the return of the deported, the prophets have promoted restoration as the end of punishment. This ideal could be regarded as the precursor of our modern understandings of imprisonment, the internal exile within one's country, that should seek the restoration and rehabilitation of the internally deported.

Scholars have also noted how early Judaism was deeply uncomfortable with capital punishment. In the Mishnah, rabbis express their opposition to capital punishment and state that a court that executes someone once in every seventy years is considered murderous.[32] Rabbinic Judaism placed lots of legal barriers, making such a sentence extremely difficult to carry out. Therefore, being the image of God is not about effecting capital punishment. It is about being aware that I am responsible for the life of the other. God's people, in every generation, through trial and error, learn to handle this sacred fire of justice, and, to the extent that they care to remain on this trajectory, they may be called God's images.

---

28. See also Knight, *Law, Power, and Justice*, 48, 143. Even in the case of the Canaanites who lived in the land before the conquest by the Israelites, Leviticus speaks of their annihilation as exile (Lev 18:28–29).

29. See also Westbrook, "Personal Exile," 322.

30. The biblical texts refer to stories where mercy always remains an option. The victim is free, if he or she wants, to give up the demand for retribution (e.g. 2 Sam 14:11).

31. Isa 4:4; 5:7; 26:21; Ezek 22:13–16; Hos 1:4; 4:2; Mic 3:10–12; 7:2. The length of time for which Israel would continue to possess their land was directly dependent upon the shedding of innocent blood on their soil (Num 35:33–34).

32. *Mishnah Makkot* 1.10.

Conclusions

"Being human is becoming increasingly humane," says John W. Rogerson.[33] Being in the image of God means that a person is charged with the burden of the world. For a long time, we have focused on the givenness of the image and we have neglected this side of non-givenness of the *imago Dei* in those who are called to exercise justice. The givenness of the *imago Dei* is actually what ancient kings relied on regardless of whether or not their responsibility towards their people was carried out. I doubt that the Scriptures wanted their readers to rely on this same givenness of the image independently of their way of being in the world. On the contrary, I believe the Scriptures issue a warning against presupposing it and self-declaring it lightly. In fact, only Jesus can adequately claim it.

When God made humans in his image, he placed us on a path of becoming increasingly humane, and in this chapter we have seen how being on this path plays out in the issue of capital justice. The path of justice is the path of Jesus Christ, and being the church means being placed on this path, the *only* path there is: learning it, failing, repenting and continuously returning to it. No other path exists for the church.

I have seen that my life and Christian identity is not separate from what happens to women in the brothels, to refugees in the camps, to the children caught in the nets of human traffickers, to the marginalized foreigners. I am not free to exclude them from my narrative; I am not free to exclude them from my theology, from my sermons, from my church activities, from my monthly budget, from my teaching. And when I serve them, I serve them for my *own* sake. I serve them so I can be regarded as "human." I have realized that it is actually arrogant to serve the disadvantaged only in order to solve *their* problem. It is arrogant to serve them so that they can be "human" just like I am. I am the one who is not human without them.

If I take seriously the whole counsel of Scripture, the teachings of the Torah and the voices of the prophets, I cannot ignore that Israel would rise and fall on the basis of how they lived with justice in their land. Israel, as God's people, could *not* exist apart from imaging God's just character. What makes us think that the church can exist without imaging God? Indeed, there are Christians who believe that Christ came to *save* them from imaging God rather than to *enable* them to image God, and that is a very dangerous conviction. Jesus's most terrifying response was: "I never knew you; go away from me" (Matt 7:23).

---

33. Rogerson, *Theology of the Old Testament*, 136.

If we are image bearers, then we have been bestowed with the extremely difficult task of navigating justice, as Genesis 9:6 has authorized, but our work is always done in awareness of its imperfection and always in anticipation of the perfect justice that can only be brought about by the perfect image of God, namely Christ himself (cf. Isa 9:6; 16:5; Ps 9:5). There is no finality in human justice, and it is dangerous to seek finality in our justice. It is always unfinished, always modest, humble and expectant; never totalized.

However, our anticipation of Christ's justice does not mean we are not to struggle with how to reflect that coming justice here on earth. I have no illusions that we will cease wars, that we will bring human trafficking to an end, that all refugees will be restored to their homes; but my small anticipatory actions are my submission to God's declaration that I be his image. At the same time, my small actions are a foretelling evangelization of what is on the way.

References

Blenkinsopp, Joseph. *Creation, De-Creation, Re-Creation: A Discursive Commentary on Genesis 1–11*. London/New York: T&T Clark, 2011.

de Vaux, Roland. *Ancient Israel*. Vol. 1, *Social Institutions*. New York: McGraw-Hill, 1965.

Dickson, D. Bruce. "Kingship as Racketeering: The Royal Tombs and Death Pits at Ur, Mesopotamia, Reinterpreted from the Standpoint of Conflict Theory." In *Experiencing Power, Generating Authority: Cosmos, Politics, and the Ideology of Kingship in Ancient Egypt and Mesopotamia*, edited by Jane A. Hill, Philip Jones and Antonio J. Morales, 311–328. Philadelphia: University of Pennsylvania Museum of Archaeology and Anthropology, 2013.

Frymer-Kensky, Tikva. "The Atrahasis Epic and Its Significance for Our Understanding of Genesis 1–9." *Biblical Archeologist* 40, no. 4 (1977): 147–155.

Gordon, Robert P. *Genesis 1–11 in Its Ancient Context*. Cambridge: Grove Books, 2015.

Holsclaw, Geoff, and Scot McKnight. "Reviewing David Bentley Hart." Patheos, 2 October 2019. https://www.patheos.com/blogs/jesuscreed/2019/10/02/reviewing-david-bentley-hart/?fbclid=IwAR0OapxeMOSTectm4xe5s7dw3D9dWxC9c371K PsQpiZklGxPrKNI6JGlnvs.

Holtz, Shalom E. "Stoning the Idolater: The Significance of Proper Procedure." The Torah.com, 2013. https://www.thetorah.com/article/stoning-the-idolater-the-significance-of-proper-procedure.

Knight, Douglas A. *Law, Power, and Justice in Ancient Israel*. Louisville, KY: Westminster John Knox, 2011.

Middleton, J. Richard. *The Liberating Image: The* Imago Dei *in Genesis 1*. Grand Rapids, MI: Brazos, 2005.

Otto, Eckart. "Human Rights: The Influence of the Hebrew Bible." *Journal of Northwest Semitic Languages* 25, no. 1 (1999): 1–20.

Priest, James E. "Gen 9:6: A Comparative Study of Bloodshed in Bible and Talmud." *Journal of the Evangelical Theological Society* 31, no. 2 (1988): 145–151.

Rogerson, John W. *A Theology of the Old Testament: Cultural Memory, Communication, and Being Human.* London: SPCK, 2009.

Stott, John. *Issues Facing Christians Today.* 4th rev. and updated ed. Grand Rapids, MI: Zondervan, 2006.

United Nations. "Universal Declaration of Human Rights." 1948. https://www.un.org/en/universal-declaration-human-rights/.

Westbrook, Raymond. "Personal Exile in the Ancient Near East." *Journal of the American Oriental Society* 128, no. 2 (2008): 317–323.

Wilson, Stephen M. "Blood Vengeance and the *Imago Dei* in the Flood Narrative (Genesis 9:6)." *Interpretation* 71, no. 3 (2017): 263–273.

Zehnder, Markus. "Cause or Value? Problems in the Understanding of Gen 9,6a." *Zeitschrift für die alttestamentliche Wissenschaft* 122, no. 1 (2010): 81–89.

4

The Gospel and the Public Square

Our Social Responsibility, as Believers and Citizens, in the World

David Zac Niringiye

It is a privilege and a joy to contribute to this celebration and exploration of *radical discipleship*, especially fitting as we together honour the global legacy of the Rev Dr John Stott. Dr Stott is one of the towering figures who guided me in my faith journey. I first met him during my formative years as a student at university, and continued the relationship through the different seasons of life and location, as friend and mentor, to the time of my ordination as a bishop in the Church of Uganda (in the Anglican tradition). Uncle John, as many of us his younger friends and mentees fondly called him, accompanied me throughout my adult life and ministry – from our first meeting in 1980, through face-to-face encounters, regular letter correspondence, and my listening to him at various conferences and closely studying his many books. In particular, I have two most cherished memories. First, during my time as a graduate student at Wheaton College, he was a featured speaker in chapel in 1987. He invited me to the back room of the chapel to pray with him before he spoke, and then he asked that I pray for him. I thought for a moment, "Me? Pray for world-renowned John Stott?" I was deeply moved by his humility. Second, we were together on a ten-day birdwatching holiday in the wild and parks of Uganda in 1999. I was amazed at his authenticity – no airs about being a celebrated global evangelical icon – as we ate, drank and laughed together, discussing theology and ministry, as well as life's twists and turns.

This essay addresses the question of the gospel mandate for believers' responsibility and engagement with critical issues and problems in society – a subject that occupied part of Stott's life and work. He is credited with having made a significant contribution to the recovery of the evangelical social conscience in the 1970s, as evidenced in "The Lausanne Covenant"[1] (of which he was the chief architect). The Covenant was clear that those who "believe the Gospel is God's good news for the whole world" and "are determined by his grace to obey Christ's commission to proclaim it to all [hu]mankind and make disciples of every nation"[2] ought to share in God's "concern for justice and reconciliation throughout human society and for the liberation of [humanity] from every kind of oppression."[3] I too was persuaded early in my faith journey that social action was integral to Christian discipleship. John Stott's two books *Christian Counter-Culture: The Message of the Sermon on the Mount* (published in 1978) and *Issues Facing Christians Today* (1984) were particularly invaluable in my formative years for grappling with the prior question as to whether there is an imperative in the gospel for social justice. *Issues Facing Christians Today* was my first public theology text. Stott's other publications that were influential in shaping my thinking were *The Cross of Christ* (1986) and *The Contemporary Christian: An Urgent Plea for Double Listening* (1992). Another critical work in this direction was the founding of the London Institute for Contemporary Christianity, "whose raison d'être is to help people develop a Christian perspective on the complexities of the modern world."[4]

It is Stott's passionate and incessant call for "double listening" – by which he meant "to listen carefully (although of course with differing degrees of respect) both to the ancient Word and to the modern world, in order to relate the one to the other with a combination of fidelity and sensitivity"[5] – which was for me the most valuable hermeneutical tool for grappling with Christian social engagement. I surmise that this was the secret of his ability to listen and engage with issues in context, including listening to others who held a different viewpoint, even on matters that he considered essential.[6] The value of "double

---

1. "The Lausanne Covenant" is a statement from the historic gathering of evangelical Christian leaders from across the geographical and ecclesiastical-theological spectrum in 150 countries, in Lausanne, Switzerland, in 1974. For a full record of its proceedings, see Douglas, *Let the Earth*.

2. Douglas, 3.

3. "The Lausanne Covenant," in Douglas, 4.

4. Stott, *Issues Facing Christians Today*, xi.

5. Stott, *Contemporary Christian*, 13.

6. The book by Edwards and Stott, *Essentials*, is one such example.

listening" is in its focusing our attention on the two essential questions: first, "What is the gospel?," which demands that we come to some understanding of the core of "God's good news to the world";[7] and second, "What is the world?," which challenges us to come to some tentative conclusion about the defining narratives of the historical-cultural context of our location – of the world that "God so loved" (John 3:16 NIV). Whatever one hears of the gospel shapes the framing of the world as its subject-object; and what people hear as the defining narratives of the world shapes their understanding of the gospel.

This essay first considers what Stott articulated as the core of the gospel and its implications for believers' "concern for justice and reconciliation throughout human society and for the liberation of [humanity]."[8] Of particular interest to us is Stott's insistence on maintaining as distinct (though integral to each other) evangelism and social concern. It is gratifying that Stott recognized and cautioned that all hearings and understandings (and therefore his own), both of the Word and of the world, are culturally conditioned: "our culture blinds, deafens and dopes us. We neither see what we ought to see in Scripture, nor hear God's Word as we should, nor feel the anger of God against evil."[9] I submit that Stott was trapped in the evangelism–social concern binary by his cultural conditioning, blinding and doping.

This essay makes a case for shifting the discourse, and proposes different language by which social justice is integral to the gospel, and social concern is integral to evangelism. There is neither need nor justification to separate the two because life is integral: the individual and community are ontologically united; and the private is public, just as the public is private. I should be clear that I have come to the conclusion that social justice is at the heart of the proclamation and demonstration of God's good news for the world. I am arguing that authentic gospel witness entails engaging with cultures, systems and structures that create the conditions of social injustice.

The Gospel Imperative for Social Justice: A Reflection on Stott's Understanding

The question "What is the gospel, according to the Scriptures?" occupied the life work of John Stott. It is therefore foolhardy to try to capture in a few paragraphs Stott's perspectives on the gospel imperative for social justice. Based

---

7. This is a subtitle in Stott's commentary, *Romans*.

8. Douglas, *Let the Earth*, 4.

9. Stott, *Contemporary Christian*, 193.

on my experience of him and of reading several of his works, I suggest four key features of the gospel narrative that Stott articulated as core to "God's good news for the whole world." I too believe that these four are the heart of the gospel.

First, God's good news is Jesus of Nazareth, God incarnate and the Christ of God. The storyline delineating this feature is what Stott called the fourfold scheme of biblical history: that "the Bible divides human history into epochs, marked by four major events – the creation, the Fall, the Redemption and the End."[10] This reading of the biblical narrative led him to conclude that there are five biblical doctrines,[11] which become the basis for Christian social engagement: a fuller doctrine of God, who created the universe and is therefore concerned for the whole of humankind and the whole of human life in all its colour and complexity; a fuller doctrine of human beings, as godlike beings made in God's likeness, and therefore with intrinsic worth and dignity, as well as fallen and depraved and capable of much evil; a fuller doctrine of Christ, in "his paradoxical fullness – his sufferings and glory, his servanthood and lordship, his lowly Incarnation and cosmic reign";[12] a fuller doctrine of salvation, as "a radical transformation in three phases, beginning at our conversion, continuing through our earthly life and brought to perfection when Christ comes";[13] and a fuller doctrine of the church, as a people called out of the world to belong to God, and sent back into the world to witness and serve.

Second, the good news Jesus proclaimed and demonstrated, explicated in his life, death, resurrection, ascension and Pentecost, embodied the kingdom of God, because in Jesus of Nazareth "the new age had dawned, and the rule of God had broken into history."[14] Stott cautioned not to separate salvation from the kingdom of God, arguing that "in the Bible these two expressions are virtual synonyms, alternative models to describe the same work of God,"[15] and therefore equated entering the kingdom of God with being saved. Salvation is therefore the participation in the kingdom of God. He wrote:

> For the kingdom of God is God's dynamic rule, breaking into human history through Jesus, confronting, combating and overcoming evil, spreading the wholeness of personal and

---

10. Stott, *Issues Facing Christians Today*, 34.
11. Stott, 15–25.
12. Stott, 21.
13. Stott, 22.
14. Stott, *Christian Counter-Culture*.
15. Stott, *Issues Facing Christians Today*, 22.

communal wellbeing, taking possession of his people in total blessing and total demand. The Church is meant to be the kingdom community, a model of what human community looks like when it comes under the rule of God, and a challenging alternative to secular society. Entering God's Kingdom is entering the new age, long promised in the Old Testament, which is also the beginning of God's new creation. Now we look forward to the consummation of the Kingdom, when our bodies, our society and our universe will all be renewed, and sin, pain, futility, disease and death will all be eradicated. Salvation is a big concept; we have no liberty to reduce it.[16]

What Stott is affirming here is that social engagement is not an add-on but rather participating in the work of the kingdom of God by those who have entered the kingdom of God, and that it is integral to the proclamation of the gospel.

Third, the central and defining event of the Christ story is the cross, because "the only authentic Jesus is the Jesus who died on the cross."[17] Stott argues repeatedly that the biblical witness attests to the death of Jesus on the cross as the central point of the Christ story, and indeed as the key to all history and therefore "the centre of the evangelical faith."[18] He is emphatic in his book *The Cross of Christ* that the "cross is the revelation of God's justice as well as his love. That is why the community of the cross should concern itself with social justice as well as loving philanthropy."[19] He adds:

Christians cannot regard with equanimity the injustices that spoil God's world and demean his creatures. Injustice must bring pain to the God whose justice flared brightly at the cross; it should bring pain to God's people too. Contemporary injustices take many forms. They are international (the invasion and annexation of foreign territory), political (the subjugation of minorities), legal (the punishment of untried and unsentenced citizens), racial (the humiliating discrimination against people on the ground of race or colour), economic (the tolerance of gross North–South inequality and the traumas of poverty and unemployment),

---

16. Stott, 23.
17. Stott, *Cross of Christ*, 46.
18. Stott, 7.
19. Stott, 292.

sexual (the oppression of women), educational (the denial of equal opportunity for all), or religious (the failure to take the gospel to the nations). Love and justice combine to oppose all these situations. If we love people, we shall be concerned to secure their basic rights as human beings, which is also the concern of justice. The community of the cross, which has truly absorbed the message of the cross, will always be motivated to action by the demands of justice and love.[20]

It is clear that for Stott, engagement in issues of social justice is integral to bearing gospel witness to the centrality of the cross of Christ (especially for evangelicals for whom the cross is central). Notably all the social injustices and maladies he highlights relate directly or indirectly to the nature, structuring and exercise of state power. Poverty and economic exploitation, repression and abuse of human rights, incessant violent conflicts resulting in the displacement of populations and refugee crises: all these are consequences of the use and abuse of state power.

Fourth, the gospel imperative for those who live by the gospel story is summed up in the earliest of Christian affirmations, "Jesus is Lord," which expresses "first a profound theological conviction about the historic Jesus and secondly a radical personal commitment to him in consequence."[21] John Stott believed that a radical commitment to Christ has both social and political dimensions: that "to confess 'Jesus is Lord' is to acknowledge him as Lord of society, even of those societies or segments of society which do not explicitly acknowledge his lordship";[22] and that "the disciples of Jesus are to respect the state, and within limits submit to it, but they will neither worship it, nor give it the uncritical support it covets. Consequently, discipleship sometimes calls for disobedience."[23] For Stott, it was clear that there may be a time when radical discipleship demands civil disobedience.

Going by Stott's articulation of the gospel narrative, one would conclude that social justice is integral to his understanding of "God's good news for the whole world." It is therefore baffling that Stott is keen to distinguish between evangelism and social concern, sticking to the classical Lausanne position that "to affirm that evangelism and social responsibility belong to each other, we

---

20. Stott, 292–293.

21. Stott, *Contemporary Christian*, 86.

22. Stott, 94.

23. Stott, 96.

are not meaning that neither can ever exist in independence of the other."[24] Although he argues in many places that the Commission of Jesus in the Gospels (Matt 28:19–20; Mark 16:15; Luke 24:47; cf. Acts 1:8) includes social as well as evangelistic responsibility, he is emphatic that evangelism is primary. He averred:

> Christians should feel an acute pain of conscience and compassion when human beings are oppressed or neglected in any way, whether what is being denied them is civil liberty, racial respect, education, medicine, employment, or adequate food, clothing and shelter. Anything which undermines human dignity should be an offense to us. But is anything so destructive to human dignity as alienation from God through ignorance or rejection of the gospel? And how can we seriously maintain that economic liberation is just as important as eternal salvation?[25]

In seeking to keep the distinction, I would argue that Stott fell into the very trap he cautioned against – narrowing the scope of the gospel and salvation.

How are we to make sense of Stott's theological imprisonment in the evangelism–social concern dichotomy? It is by interrogating and unearthing the social–cultural narratives that (in his words) "blinded, deafened and doped" him. "What was the tint on his theological lenses?" we ask. I wonder whether he was so concerned with defending the "evangel" from the "social gospel" of theological liberalism (which was the crucible of his formative years in the 1950s and 1960s) that he was constrained to recognize social justice as part of "God's good news for the world." He was certainly persuaded that the language of "mission" and "missionary" was the appropriate way of perceiving and naming the believer's place in the world. Or is it that, in spite of much effort to debunk the spiritual–secular dichotomy of the modernist worldview, he was still very much a child of his intellectual culture, which viewed the world with the sacred–secular lens? There is another controlling narrative of the modern era which may have conditioned him to this position: the Enlightenment doctrine of the autonomous self. It is noteworthy that he asserts that "before we are ready to ask the question 'What is the gospel?', we must obtain a satisfactory answer to the logically prior question, 'What is a human being?',"[26] which implies that in his mind the primary object-subject of the gospel is human

---

24. Stott, *Making Christ Known*, 180.

25. Stott, *Christian Mission*, 38.

26. Stott, *Contemporary Christian*, 31.

beings (as individuals), rather than humanity and the entire created order. I surmise that his upper-class upbringing itself, with no first-hand experience of injustice, conditioned him to the individualistic worldview and shaped his understanding of the gospel. There is a blindness that comes with privilege.

There is no doubt that Stott's deep friendship and fellowship with leaders from contexts of colonial oppression and economic exploitation contributed to his social relocation. However, physical relocation and incarnation in contexts of exploitation and oppression have a deeper impact on transforming narratives. I have wondered how his perspective would have changed if he had lived among his friends for whom poverty, persecution and other injustices were the norm. I have also wondered whether it was the socialization of empire (the British Empire and, by extension, the West), whose "milk and honey" he drank, in spite of his well-known revulsion of colonialism and its associated paternalism. Although he was aware of the seduction of empire, as is evident in his works, it is conceivable that his location (the fact that he lived his life in England and not any other country) informed his perspectives. I have come to learn over time that narratives die hard. I have often wondered what his writings and preaching would have looked like had he lived in one of the cities of the Global South or East, or if he had co-authored some of his works on social justice with his friends in politically repressed and economically exploited contexts.

I am proposing that part of the process of freeing ourselves from the evangelism–social concern separation is to hear the gospel story from brothers and sisters whose faith lives have been formed in contexts of marginalization, oppression and exploitation. One of the major lessons from these societies is that human life is integrated; that there is an indissoluble interconnectedness and interdependence of humanity, and with all other creation. Not only is it true that being human (personhood) is social – "a body-soul-in-a-community"[27] – but the social is also political. This demands a shift in language and framing of the discourse on believers' social responsibility, since there cannot be a separation of the personal, social and political. The starting point is to acknowledge that we all share in public goods and services – believers and unbelievers alike – and therefore the call is not to "mission" as though we could extricate ourselves from our shared lives, but rather to bear witness to the gospel story as we live together, as citizens of particular geographies as well as of the wider world. I suggest that the language of public life and the public square gives us a better appreciation of the integral nature of the gospel

---

27. Stott, *Issues Facing Christians Today*, 19.

in addressing all human conditions, and gives credence to "bearing witness" as the more appropriate way of elucidating the believer's response to the gospel and responsibility in the world.

Public Life, the Public Square and the State

Typically, "public life" is defined in contrast to "private life" – life in shared spaces as contrasted with life in private, that is, in the family or other private spaces. But this contradistinction not only locks us into another of the dualisms of the modern era – the public and the private – but also misses the key motif at the core: "right of access." The distinction that needs to be made is about space and resources – public or personal. I therefore distinguish the "public" from the "personal," and assert that the "personal" is contingent upon the "public": "personal" is life in spaces where the right of access and enjoyment of goods and services is personal to the holder, by virtue of kinship and acquisition; and "public" is where the right of access and enjoyment is by virtue of being a member of the wider human community, the locus of what and how people "enjoy what they have a legitimate claim to."[28] The spheres of public life are culture, religion, economics, politics, public goods and services, the environment, media, the arts and entertainment. Public life is therefore the life of individuals, families, communities and nations in shared spaces and time, and with shared resources, by virtue of being human and part of creation. It is as old as the human community. The metaphor of the "garden of Eden" in the Genesis 2 narrative is precisely about human community being in "communion with the rest of creation . . . a glorious picture of the creation-community abiding in its Creator."[29]

The notion "public square" is to do with structuring public life in a particular geography and history. It answers the "how" and "what": how different individuals, families and communities access and enjoy public space, goods and services; and what resources are apportioned to whom. Every human story, every community, is located in a particular geography and timeline. The primary geography of life together, where human beings share public spaces, goods and services (as well as other aspects of creation), is territories and countries. Countries are the spaces within which public life is regulated: within which we share spaces, goods, services and the limited resources of Planet Earth. The moderating factors of the public square are culture, politics and

---

28. Wolterstorff, *Hearing the Call*, 13.
29. Niringiye, *The Church*, 43.

economics. These three factors are interwoven. Culture shapes politics and economics; politics and economics are the drivers of the dynamic of culture; politics shape economics; and economics shape politics. The public square is the arena for managing and regulating culture, politics and economics, with a view to providing for what and how people enjoy what they have a legitimate claim to and their responsibilities in society. This is what the modern state is about: sovereignty over a defined and distinct territory, with a population and a governing authority.

The state is the contemporary locus of the exercise of public power – the organization and management of public life. The biblical narrative seems to take the notion of the state for granted in the life of societies. In fact, the apostle Paul was emphatic that state authority was established by God.[30] Nicholas Wolterstorff captures the spirit of the Scriptures in regard to the existence of the state: "States are an indispensable component of God's providential care for humankind in this time between the Resurrection and the Eschaton. States are necessary for human existence in history; they provide the order without which there could not be human existence in history."[31] States are characterized by policies and laws, domiciled in institutions, and governed by a cadre of officials, which embody culture, systems and structures for ordering public life. The nature of the state defines individual location – how individuals exercise their rights and responsibilities; how individuals enjoy what they have a legitimate claim to; creating and moderating conditions for individual and community life.

Politics is the structuring, regulating and management of power to determine access and enjoyment of public spaces, goods and services. In public life, how interdependent relationships are managed is the business of politics because, in the end, "politics *is* the means by which people create relationships to live with others."[32] It is "the distribution of power, the means of wielding it, whether for good, bad or an indifferent end."[33] Politics is always about identity; "who gets what, when, how," as the American political scientist Harold Lasswell defined politics. Citizenship is the narrative that defines what rights and responsibilities are enjoined on individuals and groups. Thus, citizenship is a political norm. And so politics impacts everyone: believers and unbelievers, consciously or unconsciously.

---

30. Rom 13:1–7.

31. Wolterstorff, *The Mighty and the Almighty*, 24.

32. Raskin, *Common Good*, 19.

33. Raskin, 19.

Social justice is therefore embodied in the ordering of public life; in culture, systems and structures, enshrined in legal and policy instruments and institutions. Injustice is therefore a matter of culture, systems and structures: the use and abuse of public power. Hence, grappling with issues of injustice demands that we address the question of the nature and character of the state because states create and moderate conditions of social justice or injustice. Poverty, the rape and abuse of nature and the environment, exploitation, social-economic inequalities, marginalization, dehumanization, and the like, are conditions created and entrenched by states and those who wield public power. The question of social justice is about the condition of life, in particular of the weak and vulnerable; transforming those conditions demands transformation of the structures of distribution of public power and therefore the state. What and how individuals and communities engage with nature and the character of the state are answered by the rights and responsibilities accorded to the people who dwell in countries – which is the question of citizenship.

Believers as Citizens in the World

The question whether there is a gospel imperative for social justice seeks to understand whether the gospel story offers a compelling narrative for transforming culture, systems and structures. Does the gospel narrative provide a framework for public values, norms and aspirations for all people, irrespective of religious and social-cultural identity or party-political affiliation? These are questions to do with the structuring of states and therefore about believers as citizens of the world. At the individual level, the question is whether the gospel narrative provides a basis for rights and responsibilities, what they are, and how a believer is to exercise them. At the level of the collective – the body of believers (a church or a group of churches, however they are structured) – it is a question of whether and what values, norms and aspirations it lives and therefore commends to other groups, in shaping the public life of all the people.

This expectation is not far-fetched, as our earlier discussion of Stott's articulation of the core elements of the gospel story has shown. Moreover, there is a coherence in the entire biblical narrative pointing to all of creation as the subject of the gospel, beginning in Genesis with the creation narratives, with God who "created the heavens and the earth [cosmos]" (Gen 1:1). The whole of creation is the arena of God's action and the ordering of all of life, as part of the story of God's purpose and plan to redeem creation. Jesus's teaching of what his disciples ought to imagine about life on earth is summarized in what we have come to know as the Lord's Prayer: "your kingdom come, your will be done, on earth as it is heaven" (Matt 6:10 NIV). While it does not prescribe any particular form of state, the narrative seems consistent that, whatever form it takes, the state ought to provide for the right of all to "enjoy what they have a legitimate claim to." However, the consistent picture in the Scriptures is that while the public square (the ordering of public life) is instituted by God, more often than not those in authority capture it and turn it into an instrument of their greed and folly.

Romans 13:1–7 has been for me an important passage in my journey of resisting and encouraging others to resist injustices and the abuse of power by those who are entrusted with political power. Sadly, it is a passage that has been misread and misinterpreted as teaching that all people who run governments hold power by the will of God. But Paul distinguishes "governing authorities" (the state) from those who are "in authority" (the state's official representatives). Fusing "governing authority" and those "in authority" gives divine legitimacy to any governments irrespective of what they do with the power they steward. Paul is clear that "the one in authority is God's servant for your good" (Rom 13:4 NIV); in other words, those who govern are accountable to God and ought to use the power they wield for the good of society and upholding social justice.

Consider for a moment that the immediate first-century readers of Romans were a marginal, despised and persecuted community of Jesus people. Even as marginal a community as they were, they had the right to expect from the Roman rulers what was due to them – their good. Paul was saying to them that they ought to obey those in authority as they stewarded power according to the will of God – for the good of society; and, by implication, they ought to resist and disobey them when they undermined that mandate. Stott said it well: "We are to submit right up to the point where obedience to the state would entail disobedience to God. But if the state commands what God forbids, or forbids what God commands, then our plain Christian duty is to resist, not to submit, to disobey the state in order to obey God."[34]

We should recall the apostles' bold response when those in the Jewish ruling council ordered them to stop teaching in Jesus's name: "We must obey God rather than human beings!" (Acts 5:29). The apostles defied the Sanhedrin's order, because to obey it was tantamount to disobeying God.

I submit that the most urgent discourse today, for us as believers in a world where injustice has become the norm, is the question of believers as citizens in the world. Indeed, "Blessed are those who hunger and thirst for righteousness, for they will be filled" (Matt 5:6 NIV).

---

34. Stott, *Romans*, 342.

References

Douglas, J. D. (ed). *Let the Earth Hear His Voice: International Congress on World Evangelization, Lausanne, Switzerland.* Minneapolis, MN: World Wide, 1975.

Edwards, David L., and John Stott. *Essentials: A Liberal–Evangelical Dialogue.* London/Sydney/Auckland/Toronto: Hodder & Stoughton, 1988.

Niringiye, David Zac. *The Church: God's Pilgrim People.* Downers Grove, IL: InterVarsity Press, 2015.

Raskin, Marcus G. *The Common Good: Its Politics, Policies and Philosophy.* New York: Routledge & Kegan Paul, 1986.

Stott, John R. W. *Christian Counter-Culture: The Message of the Sermon on the Mount.* Downers Grove, IL: InterVarsity Press; Leicester: Inter-Varsity Press, 1978.

———. *Christian Mission in the Modern World.* Downers Grove, IL: InterVarsity Press, 2008.

———. *The Contemporary Christian: An Urgent Plea for Double Listening.* Leicester: Inter-Varsity Press, 1992.

———. *The Cross of Christ.* Downers Grove, IL: InterVarsity Press; Leicester: Inter-Varsity Press, 1986.

———. *Issues Facing Christians Today.* London: Marshall, Morgan & Stott, 1984.

———. *Romans: God's Good News for the World.* Downers Grove, IL: InterVarsity Press, 1994.

Stott, John (ed.). *Making Christ Known: Historic Documents from the Lausanne Movement 1974–1989.* Carlisle: Paternoster, 1996.

Wolterstorff, Nicholas. *Hearing the Call: Liturgy, Justice, Church, and World.* Grand Rapids, MI: Eerdmans, 2011.

———. *The Mighty and the Almighty: An Essay in Political Theology.* Cambridge: Cambridge University Press, 2012.

5

Relentless Love and Justice in Radical Whole-Life Discipleship

Jason Fileta

John Stott was a radical disciple – the gospel informed every aspect of his life. His commitment to the gospel was not to a set of tasks on a checklist, a garment to wear on Sunday morning or a list of moral chores to complete. The reality of the gospel and the implications of Jesus's coming reign permeated life itself. Where did this radical discipleship lead Dr Stott? It led him to care for the environment, to care for the poor, to boldly challenge injustice, and to live deeply meaningful relationships with Christians in the Global South.

This is not the dominant paradigm of North American Christianity. If radical discipleship were the norm, then we would not need to intentionally reflect on John Stott's life and consider how these pressing questions around caring for creation, the poor and oppressed, and global Christianity were integral to his life as a disciple. But our models of engaging with these critical issues have been influenced more by our culture than by Scripture and the Spirit. We have made the gospel so bare that somehow it is possible to believe it, to live by it and to accept it while remaining neutral to injustice, unconcerned about the care of creation, and isolated from our global brothers and sisters in the faith. To supplement this scarce meal we have made pursuing justice for the poor and oppressed a side dish: justice as a project. I will call this paradigm "domesticated love."

Domesticated Love Makes Justice a Project

I am the first to admit that those who have perpetuated "justice as a project" the most are people like me, those who work in Christian NGOs whose entire purpose is to alleviate suffering and to respond to injustice. We made justice a project because it is easier to market that way. We have inspired people with Scripture and with stories of injustice and of hope and transformation. We have prayed mightily for apathy to end. And then, after we have stirred people's souls and inspired folk to join our movements, we have asked them to subcontract the project to us. We have created a system built on both conviction and convenience. We want justice to be a commodity that we can sell you on Amazon, and like the other products you buy it must have a low barrier to entry, low cost, and low demand on you. We do not want to interrupt comfort and convenience, we just want to share in the benefits . . . and this has worked well enough to perpetuate the model. There is no doubt that good work has happened. God has used our meagre offerings, and he has transformed communities. Some slaves have been set free, some chains have been broken, some hungry have been fed. But it is not enough. It is a grave mistake for those of us who work in the field of international justice to mobilize our supporters in such a way as to encourage them to maintain lifestyles sustained by the oppression of others as long as they give a 10 percent kickback. This framework must be challenged.

It is time to be honest: our response to poverty, injustice, and a creation that is groaning cannot be contained to a once-a-year giving or a 10 percent threshold. It may be easy to contain our engagement with a hurting world, but it cheapens the call to discipleship. This not only robs the world of radical and bold love, but it robs us of deeply meaningful relationships with our brothers and sisters around the world, and the peace and joy that come from seeing God's redemption unfold before our own eyes. It prevents us from wrestling with difficult questions, from working out our faith with fear and trembling, and from having to *live* radically.

Love that is domesticated is largely oriented around one's own achievement and uprightness. It shows just enough compassion to those in need because it is the right thing to do – but this type of "love in action" tends to lack deep roots. It tends to be performative, and does not require one to examine the most fundamental truths about injustice. Domesticated love creates just enough good to keep us from wholeheartedly rejecting evil.

I will never forget hearing Vinoth Ramachandra, a Sri Lankan senior leader in the International Fellowship of Evangelical Students (IFES), speak at the 2012 Micah Network Global Consultation. Talking about partnership in development, he said that if you show up in Sri Lanka with a bag of money and an idea, people will tell you it's an amazing idea and they just cannot wait to work on it. You will then think that this is community-led development, or that it is partnership, but no: you have merely turned up with your ideas in a place where we are so desperate for survival that someone is going to tell you it's a wonderful idea and exactly what we need to do simply to access resources of any kind. Justice as a project not only cheapens the experience of those who feel the conviction to fight injustice, but it really does not do the good it could be doing in the field around the world. We cannot continue with this model.

We have seen the fruit of this model in North America. Many of my friends have walked away from their faith because it did not seem to be relevant. So many people have been burdened by a world filled with poverty, injustice and environmental degradation, and have somehow come to believe that following Jesus says nothing about this burden. We made it possible to follow Jesus and have nothing to say about injustice. Domesticated love with justice as a project is not enough.

Justice as a project allows us to draw a red X for anti-slavery on one hand and then purchase goods made by slaves with our right hand.

Justice as a project allows us to vote for politicians and celebrate policies that completely devastate the environment and perpetuate climate change, but then quickly give money to support the children of impoverished farmers no longer able to grow food because of our climate crisis.

Justice as a project allows us to mobilize blankets and backpacks of supplies for people who are fleeing conflict as refugees, but then also celebrate when our government closes the door to admitting refugees into our own nation.

These are the fruits of justice as a project – it is very incomplete. Things ostensibly done to benefit others are often designed around what would most benefit us, and it is as easy as possible. This is a far cry from Dr Stott's own radical discipleship. How did we get here? I do not believe we got here all on our own. I believe actual sinister evil has been at work, because I do not know how else to explain that amidst the greatest migration and refugee crisis in recent history, 80 percent of evangelical Christians in my nation are celebrating the slashing of refugee admittance to our nation.

One thing we have done to contribute to domesticating love is that we have taken the ocean of sin that infects our world, and reduced immense evil to simple questions of personal piety. Our notions of sin have been so personal that our ideas of redemption are similarly personal. We have failed to see the sins of systems, of culture, of nations. Therefore, we do not think God's redemption has to touch those things. This is the beauty of our God: the God who is so deeply concerned with the slavery of his people in Egypt is also deeply concerned with my small life. Sin is both personal and systemic, and so are the reaches of God's redemption. Let us explore the implications of redemptive, relentless love when it seeps throughout our lives and society.

Relentless Love Integrates Justice into Every Aspect of Life

A colleague of mine sent me a pamphlet written by Dr Stott for Tearfund in 1976. Stott wrote this pamphlet, *Walk in His Shoes: The Compassion of Jesus*, for our organization to accompany a filmstrip Tearfund had made and was taking on a tour of churches in the UK. Every paragraph is gold. It was difficult to pull out just one quote, but the following passage illuminates how Dr Stott looked to Jesus as his model for seeing others, hearing others, and responding with radical love:

> The good works Jesus did are not to be understood only as evidences of the arrival of God's reign and of the decline of the devil's dominion. They were also, and primarily, plain works of compassion. "Compassion" is often attributed to Jesus by the Gospel writers; this was the supreme motive behind his service. He was deeply moved by the sight of human need, moved with compassion and therefore moved to action. If I give some examples, the pattern will quickly emerge. In nearly every case it was a physical condition which aroused Jesus' concern . . .
>
> Whether it was the crowd or an individual, the sequence was the same. First, "he saw." True love is always observant, and the eyes of Jesus never missed the sight of need. Nobody could accuse him of being like the priest and Levite in his parable of the Good Samaritan. Of both it is written, "he saw him." Yet each saw him without seeing, for he looked the other way, and so "passed by on the other side." Jesus, on the other hand, truly "saw." He was not afraid to look human need in the face, in all its ugly reality. And what he saw invariably moved him to compassion, and so to compassionate service. Sometimes, he spoke. But his compassion never dissipated itself in words; it found expression in deeds. He saw, he felt, he acted. The movement was from the eye to the heart, and from the heart to the hand. His compassion was always aroused by the sight of need, and it always led to constructive action.[1]

---

1. Stott, *Walk in His Shoes*, 4–8.

Jesus's compassion "never dissipated itself in words." I love that description. Jesus's compassion always led to action. I wish we could make that part of the terms of service of Twitter: that we would never be deceived into believing that our words are enough. It is a system of convenience that produces activism that is measured by likes and retweets rather than policy or behaviour change. This is markedly different from the deep compassion Jesus had that always found action. Let us turn to the teachings of Jesus to explore further the significance of action.

I want to look at the teaching of Jesus in Matthew 25, what we typically call "The Parable of the Sheep and the Goats." In that same 1976 pamphlet Dr Stott refers to this teaching and says, "The passage is sometimes called 'The Parable of the Sheep and the Goats.' It is not a parable, however. The only element in it which is clearly parabolic or figurative is the likening of the saved and the lost to sheep and goats. Apart from this, it appears to be a straight and very solemn account of the final judgment."[2] Jesus says that whatever we have done to the hungry, the thirsty, the stranger, the sick, the naked and the imprisoned we have done to him. Jesus is not being inspirational with these words. Typically I hear this passage used inspirationally: "Imagine that the hungry, the thirsty, the stranger, the sick, the naked, and the imprisoned are Jesus and treat them as you would treat your Saviour." Instead, he is saying something that we do not even have words in the English language to describe: he is saying, "When you feed the hungry, you feed me." What Jesus is describing here is something I have come to call a "mystical solidarity." Jesus is describing a level of true solidarity, such that he literally experiences the comfort and the pain of the most vulnerable in our world. It is truly mystical.

In Christ we see the opposite of the paradigm I was describing earlier, in which love is domesticated and justice is contained in a series of one-off projects. The new paradigm is this: Christ's love is not domesticated but relentless; and his concern for justice permeates everything. How do we move from this first framework towards a framework of relentless love? There are a few ways we can allow this framework to take hold of our lives, but it requires a reimagining of what it looks like to "do justice" and what it means to be a disciple.

We must rely on God's power, not on our performance or activities. Awakenings to the implications of whole-life discipleship – the relentless love and lifestyle of justice – are often quickly followed by burnout, disillusionment and disappointment. As we begin to unravel injustice, we realize how deeply

---

2. Stott, 19.

it permeates everything. It becomes clear that to simply exist in this world we are participants in fallen systems that oppress and injure beloved children of God and his creation. To avoid this, it is critical to always remember two things: we will not save the world; and God is saving and will save. I have found prayer to be the most important anchor to help me remember that I am not God, allowing those burdens that are only for him to remain with him, but also helping me to stay focused on my calling as Jesus's disciple. I have also found myself coming back again and again to the promise of God in Revelation 21: that one day, when Jesus reigns, there will be no more suffering, no more death, no more poverty, no more injustice. All things will be made new, even the rest of creation. The evangelistic implications of this have surprised me – more often than not I find myself preaching the gospel and declaring who God is when I am declaring how things were meant to me, and one day will be. When we look at a world in which climate change has plunged 29 million people into hunger because they cannot grow food, it is a chance to also say that God never intended it to be this way. Every denouncing of injustice is an opportunity to announce the character and promises of God.

In this new paradigm of relentless love we must be humble, institutionally humble. We must be willing to orient our actions around what those most impacted by injustice are telling us matters most to them – even when this departs from what we want to do. If we go back to the account from Dr Ramachandra where he described typical aid programmes and essentially said we should not show up with a bag of money and an idea to "help," what he did suggest to us instead was very uncomfortable. He said that when he and others are detained or imprisoned for naming human rights abuses, the government says, "If the Americans can do this in Iraq, then why can't we?" He went on to say that what would really help his community would be if the US church filled the streets in protest over our own nation's human rights abuses and state violence so that other nations could no longer hide behind our nation's actions. This is a far cry from sponsoring a child or building a well. This is uncomfortable for many of us, but we must be willing to *listen* and *act accordingly*.

Finally, this new paradigm will lead us down paths we never could have anticipated – ways of living that seek to honour God, his creation and his most vulnerable children. We will begin to see that discipleship means we seek to live justly – not just "do justice" in limited, discrete actions. It will cause us to be curious about the things we buy, where they came from and who made them. It will cause us to examine the way we vote, our leaders and our nation's policies in a new way. It will cause us to make new choices about banking and investing.

It will even reach into our most intimate moments with God and influence how we pray, what we pray for, and for whom we pray. This may sound like a recipe for an exhausting list of dos and don'ts, which is why this paradigm shift must be deeply rooted in regular reminders of who God is, and what it means to follow him in all areas and facets of life. If we believe that God is just, that God longs to see this world renewed, and that God never intended people to die from hunger, violence, poverty and preventable disease, then every single act we do to prevent those things from happening is an act of worship. It is an act of defiance against the kingdom of this world, and welcoming worship for God's kingdom to come.

I find it totally illogical but completely transformative that God wants us to participate in the bringing in of his kingdom. He doesn't need us. He created this world, and he will redeem it, but by design he has invited us into a radical life – to join him in his redemptive work. I think that is perhaps one of the greatest joys of following Jesus: we get to be a part of this world's transformation.

In closing, it has become clear to me that radical discipleship will have two major markers: it will cost something, and it will bring transformation. If our discipleship maintains our comfort, wealth and power, or brings no real change in this world, then we must ask ourselves if we are disciples of Jesus, or rather disciples of our culture. John Stott modelled radical discipleship, and it was on display in a life oriented around relentless love for the most vulnerable in our world, the rest of God's creation, and deep relationships with Christians in the Global South. My prayer is that we too will wrestle with our own discipleship in our own contexts, and come to live justly because we love relentlessly.

Reference

Stott, John R. W. *Walk in His Shoes: The Compassion of Jesus.* London: Inter-Varsity Press, 1976.

Part 3

Creation Care

6

Intertwining Roots for Just Conviviality

Ruth Padilla DeBorst

He was addicted. He confessed, "[I am] addicted to the observation of wildlife in general and birds in particular."[1] About his visit to the Galapagos Islands, where he studied and photographed iguanas, tortoises, albatrosses, frigate birds and many other animals, he wrote, "I had an orgy of photography."[2] Undoubtedly, if he were alive today, he would be grieving deeply for the three billion birds that have disappeared in the last fifty years in North America, and at the tragic news about accelerated global warming.[3] Meet John Stott, or "Tío Juan" as we knew him in Latin America, the pastor-teacher who taught us to look and to listen. To look, to see the beauty of creation, to see through the eyes of others. To listen, to hear the song of birds, to listen to the Word of God and to what was going on in the world.

Now this chapter does not intend to promote addictions or orgies – unless they are of the sort Stott embodied! Instead, it invites us to explore the interconnectedness of creation, to acknowledge our need for interdependence in the global church, and to take steps towards mutual accountability within this web of life: intertwining roots for just conviviality.

First, as usual, in true Latin American fashion, I bring you greetings. Greetings from your sisters and brothers at Casa Adobe, the intentional Christian community in Costa Rica where my husband and I, along with an

---

1. Stott, "How the Author Became a Bird-Watcher," 13.
2. Dudley-Smith, *John Stott*, 200.
3. Cornell University, "New Study"; GrrlScientist, "Bye-Bye Birdies."

unlikely assortment of people from many different countries, are seeking to live in right relations with one another, with our human neighbours, and with the rest of creation. And greetings from CETI, the Community of Interdisciplinary Theological Studies, a learning community that seeks to nourish radical discipleship across Latin America.

Next, a word about the metaphor that permeates this entire chapter: giant redwood trees. The giant redwoods can grow for a thousand years to enormous heights, and one would expect that each particular tree would have very strong, deep roots to support such a size. However, the roots of individual trees are surprisingly small. These impressive trees can stand and grow thanks to the fact that their roots are intertwined in an intimate network that sustains and nourishes them all. The trees nearer the river send nutrients through their roots to trees further away from the sources of water. They function as a living, mutually sustaining community. I suggest that in a world bent on limitless and unsustainable economic growth with all its ecological fall-outs, in a world in which leaders and churches are also enticed to grow unsustainably, pursuing status, wealth and image, and leaving behind many excluded people, the challenge that faces followers of Jesus from North and South, East and West, is to set aside those enticements and instead allow God's Spirit to weave us into God's community of intertwined roots of radical discipleship, as citizens of God's kingdom and promoters of just conviviality.

Here we are, in the year 2020. Media waves are swirling: more and more species are becoming extinct; the world is getting hotter even faster than predicted, generating more intense hurricanes, longer droughts and record-breaking heat; entire populations are being forced to migrate for lack of sustenance.[4] It is ever more impossible to deny the impact of human activity on the planet, and this has led ours to be termed the Anthropocene era, one in which human beings are a major geological force, negatively affecting all the planetary systems.[5] As the September 2019 UN Climate Action Summit in New York revealed, and in spite of massive demonstrations and the courageous denunciation of Greta Thunberg, relatively few state and business leaders appear to be listening, let alone ready to change the policies and practices that are exacerbating the crisis. Indigenous peoples, so often judged as primitive, have been sounding the alarm for decades regarding the layers of death sown by "developed" nations on the non-human life system. Many of their vocal leaders have been murdered. And still very few listen. With few exceptions,

---

4. See, for example, Podesta, "Climate Crisis."

5. See Altvater, "The Capitalocene," 142.

evangelical leaders tend to see these matters as political and consequently unrelated to the calling of Christians in the world.

"What way forward?" we ask in pain. If not complicit denial or hopeless resignation, what is our role as followers of Jesus in this scenario? Space allows only for a couple of signposts, inspired by the life and ministry of John Stott, that can help us forge a way forward as members of the creation community and radical followers of the Lord of life.

First, we need to learn to *see*, so that we might acknowledge how intertwined we are within the biotic community. I looked towards where he pointed, but all I could see was sandy desert and scraggly, dry bushes. I was about to turn away when something suddenly moved and caught my eye. The armadillo scuttled off hurriedly as my siblings and I oohed and aahed. Tío Juan smiled. You see, during those days when we camped together in the Argentine Patagonia, John Stott taught us to look. To look up and admire birds in flight. Also, to look down, and appreciate less dramatic, small things, creatures peeking out of their hideouts in unexpected places at least expected times. Through his example and mild prodding, he taught us to see and appreciate what otherwise would have been non-existent to us. His book *The Birds Our Teachers: Essays in Orni-Theology* records the lessons he learned from birds, through patient, loving observation, about life, faith, joy, trust and perseverance.

We may not be avid birdwatchers, and we may be so blinded by our ever-lit screens that we do not realize how intricately we are tied to the rest of creation and to the birds Tío Juan so loved. But with each bird that disappears, a thread is pulled out of the delicate weaving of life. Birds not only enliven the world with their song and colour, they also consume harmful insects and weeds that threaten crops. Without them, plagues of insects would knock out the agriculture on which we depend for sustenance. Many animals – including humans – live off birds, and plants depend on them for pollination. Leonardo Boff says, "Everything that exists, co-exists . . . subsists by means of an infinite web of all-inclusive relations."[6] As thread after thread is yanked out, life itself unravels. Seeing leads us to acknowledge that we all need one another in this delicate balance of life!

Second, we need to learn to *listen*: to listen to one another and to the groaning of creation. Expectant waiting, patient searching and respectful engagement marked Uncle John's posture, not only when listening to his teachers, the birds, and to other wonders of God's creation, but also when relating to sisters and brothers of the church outside the powerful nations

---

6. Boff, *Ecology and Liberation*, 7.

of his day. This posture allowed him to tune into and appreciate unexpected contributions from unexpected places. Hardly might one expect, in our classist and racist world order, that a Cambridge-educated British clergyman might feel he had much to learn from people outside the UK. Yet Uncle John's was the humble posture of the lifelong learner. He allowed his reading of Scripture and his theological articulations to be coloured by his friendships with Christians from Africa and Latin America and the realities of their contexts. His friendship with my family began in the early 1960s and it grew through his several visits to Latin America where, along with my dad (René Padilla), he taught preaching seminars and explored several ecosystems. Although John gave my dad a nice pair of binoculars, I'm afraid he did not succeed in converting my father to his "addiction" of birdwatching; yet René's appreciation for creation *was* expanded through John's enthusiasm, and he too has become a vocal articulator of creation care as an integral part of the mission of Christians in the world.

Meanwhile, and along the two-way street stretched by the Spirit between them, John's vision of mission was expanded to become more holistic as he listened to his friends from around the world and looked at it through their eyes. In *Christian Mission in the Modern World*, he explained how he had come to shift from a focus on the Great Commission recorded in Matthew 28 to John's rendition of Jesus's prayer, which emphasizes that Christians are sent into the world, as Jesus was, not merely to preach and teach, but to express the gospel in all areas of life.[7] Significant in that broadening understanding of mission were his experiences with Christian leaders who were seeking to follow Jesus faithfully in contexts of poverty, dictatorships and violence. So, when the evangelical credentials of those leaders were questioned by the "evangelical establishment" of the North Atlantic in global fora like Lausanne I, Stott stood firmly by their side.[8] One cannot but suspect that, without Stott's active advocacy, Billy Graham's words when looking back on the Lausanne Congress might never have been uttered: "If one thing has come through loud and clear it is that we evangelicals should have social concern. The discussion in smaller groups about the contemporary meaning of radical discipleship has caught fire."[9] Humble listening had enabled Stott to mediate between sectors and to allow the gifts of the global church to be brought to the common table for mutual learning and more faithful living.

---

7. Dudley-Smith, *John Stott*, 242.

8. See Dudley-Smith, 215, and Salinas, "The Beginnings."

9. Gill, "Christian Social Responsibility," 90.

Insightful looking and respectful listening: two sensory and spiritual gifts so lacking in our fast-paced world, bent as it is on exploitation and rapid gain. Both are essential and urgent practices if we are to correct our trajectory as humanity in our common home.

¿Volverán las golondrinas? Will the swallows return to Central America? That question serves as the title of a book published in Costa Rica over forty years ago by the Swedish-Ecuadorean ecologist Ingemar Hedstrom. The recent study of bird decline cited earlier indicates that these evocative birds, whose astounding memory allows them to find the very nest in which they cracked their shell at birth, even if it is six thousand miles away and only returned to on their next migration, are severely endangered. Many of them count prominently among those three billion birds that have disappeared over the last decades, due mostly to pesticides and global warming. Will the swallows return? The answer is "no." They will not return unless we take off our consumerist glasses through which we see a dollar sign on everything – and everyone – and instead use binoculars that expose the dark shadow of deadly greed under the varnish of progress and prosperity. They will not return unless we listen to the communities already being affected by rising sea levels, desertification and ocean pollution. They will not return unless we hear the groans of the land gouged open for the extraction of the black gold it has taken millennia to produce, and work together to create alternative sources of energy. They will not return unless as Christians we go back to Scripture and allow God's Spirit to read us into the story of a good creation and a renewed earth, and we hear afresh our original calling to care for the garden in which God planted us. They will not return unless we quiet our hearts enough to hear the still, small voice of God's Spirit pleading: "Choose life!" and join with like-hearted children, women and men, not as messiahs but as humble followers of a humble Lord to live the whole gospel and make daily choices of care within the creation community.

These are lessons we are learning a day at a time at Casa Adobe. Three final stories illustrate how recognizing ourselves as part of a global body with intertwined roots can nourish our hopeful commitment and enable us to live more justly as part of that community.

For Lent last year we determined to get truly serious about reducing single-use plastic. We began trying out alternatives: cloth bags, solid containers, making our own toothpaste, and so on. One day, as we were running out of steam, I noticed that Ruth Valerio, from Tearfund, had begun a Facebook group named "Plastic-Less Living." Tuning in to the questions and experiments of sisters and brothers across the ocean gave us fresh ideas and much encouragement.

We were not alone in our effort! Instead, our modest attempts could inspire others, and many small initiatives could add up and bring some needed change.

In a similar vein, early last year, headed up by Erika Alvarez, Casa Adobe began organizing the neighbourhood to recognize our relationship with the river that runs a scarce four hundred metres from our home. Today, it is classified as the most polluted river in Central America; yet our forty-year-old neighbours remember family picnics by the river and swimming in it. A young South African volunteer has designed an artistic rendition and neighbours have written songs and poetry about the river. All these initiatives, along with regular visits to the sites and clean-up days, are allowing our neighbours to regain their relationship with the Virilla River and to make concrete commitments, such as no longer dumping trash down the side of the hill. As that relationship is healed, so are relationships within the community: people who barely nodded to one another in passing are now joined by the care for their shared place.

Finally, a confession. We began noticing some stray bees around one corner of the house. We initially tried to shoo them away. But as the days wore on, we began hearing an increasingly loud buzz. We called a local beekeeper, who offered to take care of the situation for free in exchange for the bees. Imagine our surprise when he removed the floorboard from the second storey and uncovered a huge beehive, complete with a couple of pints of honey! As he looked at the grounds and garden of Casa Adobe, and although he could have profited by taking them, he said: "I won't take the bees. This is a good home for them!" He helped us set up a proper space for them and has visited them a few times to coach our garden team about their care. All this has certainly challenged us to be far better listeners to the non-human community of which we are a part!

Will the swallows return? We cannot avoid the question if we seek to fulfil our creation mandate. To what and to whom are we listening? What do we need to see? *Whom* do we need to see? Will the swallows return? It will be an uphill battle. The answer ultimately depends on our openness to God's Spirit, who yearns to weave us into a story much larger than our individual ones, so that we may recognize ourselves as members of a living system of intertwined roots that nourishes and requires radical followership of Jesus. May we have eyes to see and ears to hear!

References

Altvater, Elmer. "The Capitalocene, or, Geoengineering against Capitalism's Planetary Boundaries." In *Anthropocene or Capitalocene? Nature, History and the Crisis of Capitalism*, edited by Jason W. Moore, 138–152. Oakland, CA: PM, 2016.

Boff, Leonardo. *Ecology and Liberation: A New Paradigm*. Maryknoll, NY: Orbis, 1995.

Cornell University. "New Study Finds US and Canada Have Lost More Than 1 in 4 Birds in the Past 50 Years." Phys.org. 19 September 2019. https://phys.org/news/2019-09-canada-lost-birds-years.html.

Dudley-Smith, Timothy. *John Stott: A Global Ministry; A Biography – The Later Years*. Downers Grove, IL: InterVarsity Press, 2001.

Gill, Athol. "Christian Social Responsibility." In *The New Face of Evangelicalism*, edited by C. René Padilla, 87–102. Downers Grove, IL: InterVarsity Press, 1976.

GrrlScientist. "Bye-Bye Birdies: Almost 3 Billion Birds Disappeared from North America's Skies in Less Than 50 Years." Forbes. 23 September 2019. https://www.forbes.com/sites/grrlscientist/2019/09/23/bye-bye-birdies-almost-3-billion-birds-disappeared-from-north-americas-skies-in-less-than-50-years/#228778724d12.

Hedstrom, Ingemar. ¿*Volverán las Golondrinas? La Reintegración de la Creación desde una Perspectiva Latinoarmericana*. San José: DEI, 1988.

Podesta, John. "The Climate Crisis, Migration and Refugees." Brookings Blum Roundtable on Global Poverty. 25 July 2019. https://www.brookings.edu/research/the-climate-crisis-migration-and-refugees/.

Salinas, Daniel. "The Beginnings of the Fraternidad Teológica Latinoamericana: Courage to Grow." *Journal of Latin American Theology: Christian Reflections from the Latino South* 1 (2006): 73–105.

Stott, John. "How the Author Became a Bird-Watcher, a Christian and a Landowner." In David Cranston, *John Stott and the Hookses*, 13. Oxford: Word by Design, 2017.

7

Loving Our Neighbour in God's World

Kuki (Lalbiakhlui) Rokhum

Introduction: Snowy Owls and Christian Discipleship

In 1997, I sat with a small group of people from different countries listening to Rev Dr John Stott tell his story about his quest to see the snowy owl. Clicking an old-style slide presenter, John Stott projected pictures of beautiful snowy owls onto the screen in front of us. This was one of those special gatherings that we had on Wednesday evenings as students of the "Christians in the Modern World" course at the London Institute of Contemporary Christianity (LICC). As a young volunteer from overseas working in a church in Southall, West London, I was captivated by his story and his photos, but I did not fully grasp his excitement at seeing and capturing photos of the snowy owl. More than twenty years later, having grown in my faith and understanding of God and Scripture, I realize that being able to see the snowy owl was not just a hobby that was fulfilled for John Stott – it revealed his deep concern for God's world and his understanding of how we are to live as disciples of Christ. In my own faith journey and through life experience, I have also been challenged to come to a deeper understanding of what it means to live as God's people in God's world. Over this time I have come to believe that there are two keys areas that demand urgent reflection and response from the global church today: first, how we understand God's relationship to the world; and second, how we understand the command to love our neighbour.

Christian Formation

I come from a small state in the north-east corner of India called Mizoram. Evangelized by Welsh missionaries in the late 1800s, Mizoram became one of those classic cases of mass evangelism where whole communities and villages gave up their animistic beliefs to embrace Christianity. Mizoram is still predominantly Christian, with 87 percent of Mizos classifying themselves as such in the 2011 census. Sunday school, memory verses, church services, vacation Bible school, daily family devotions, church choir and praying for missionaries were all regular and important parts of our family life, as they were for many Mizo families. Although our "souls" and being "good" seemed to be of prime importance in our Christian upbringing, I also distinctly remember my father's compassion for animals and his care for plants and trees.

Growing up in India, we lived fairly sustainable lives. Every single item in the home was reused and food waste was strongly frowned upon. Paper and other recyclable items were and are still sold to "rag merchants." We never had to be told to reuse plastic bags or empty bottles. Soft drinks came in glass bottles that had to be returned when finished. Everyone lived like this; hence, I believe, church teaching never really focused on how and why it is important to take care of God's earth. Our understanding of mission was largely concerned with verbal proclamation and church growth. This was and is typical, not only of the Mizo community, but also of wider India.

The Journey Continues of Knowing a "Bigger God"

My first exposure to formal biblical education was at the LICC. At that time I was working as a lay volunteer at St George's Church in Southall, West London, and was sent to LICC to do the ten-week "Christians in the Modern World" course. I learned how to engage with the Bible in its context and how we are to understand it in our contemporary context. John Stott's teaching on "double listening" was inspirational – he taught us to read the Word and listen to the world. The location of LICC was intentional – right at the heart of the city of London. The vision was that LICC would be located where the people are; we would be right in the midst of the world and not tucked away in a nice country cottage learning about the "world" and then coming out from there to "engage." My faith was opening up from just the "navel gazing" relationship between God and me.

An important experience during this time was living with Rev Dave Bookless[1] and his family and working alongside him at St George's Church. During this time I saw the Bookless family stirring in their passion for the environment. At St George's Church, we ran Holiday Bible Clubs on creation care, discovered little creepy crawlies as we took the children for walks in the local park and indulged in "pond dipping." It was about this time that A Rocha,[2] a Christian organization engaging communities in conservation, was also starting to set itself up in the UK – in the very home where I was living. It was fascinating to see this international group engaging with Scripture and passionate about the conservation of nature. Although I did not grasp the full rationale behind what they were doing, I thought it was an amazing initiative – working to redeem dirty, poisonous land, educating others about it, and adopting simple lifestyle changes.

A few years later, as a student at All Nations Christian College in Hertfordshire, my understanding of theology continued to deepen. I noticed that creation care was somewhat sidelined in discussions about mission. In our "Theology of Mission" module in 2001, environmental Christian organizations were referred to as "one form of mission." This led me to ask: Was it indeed just one aspect of mission to which just a few were called to be involved, or was it part of our very faith? All these experiences continued to reveal to me that God is much bigger than the God of my Sunday school. I was coming to a greater understanding of God's plan and purpose for the world and his love for all of creation. I was also beginning to grasp what it means to "image" God.

Towards an Integral Understanding of Mission

On returning to India, I joined a faith-based relief and development NGO called EFICOR (the Evangelical Fellowship of India Commission on Relief). EFICOR started in 1967 as a response by the Evangelical Fellowship of India (EFI) to drought in the East Indian state of Bihar. The decision taken by EFI was momentous, as in the past it had always been engaged solely in church-

---

1. Rev Dave Bookless is Director of Theology for A Rocha International (www.arocha.org). He is author of *Planetwise: Dare to Care for God's World* (Nottingham: Inter-Varsity Press, 2008) and *God Doesn't Do Waste: Redeeming the Whole of Life* (Nottingham: Inter-Varsity Press, 2010).

2. A Rocha (www.arocha.org) is an international Christian organization engaging in scientific research, environmental education and community-based conservation projects across six continents.

growth work. In 1979, leaders from within EFICOR decided that a key element of responding to the needs of the world is to educate and equip the church. EFICOR has also been engaged in influencing other organizations and movements, including the Micah Network, now known as Micah Global.[3] This is a movement and network of evangelical organizations that aims to teach and educate the Christian community about a broader understanding of mission and to help bridge the dichotomous understanding of "mission" – something that John Stott himself voiced clearly in the 1974 Lausanne Covenant.[4] After much deliberation and discussion, the Micah Declaration was released in 2001, and the term "integral mission" was used: "Integral mission or holistic transformation is the proclamation and demonstration of the gospel. It is not simply that evangelism and social involvement are to be done alongside each other. Rather, in integral mission our proclamation has social consequences as we call people to love and repentance in all areas of life. And our social involvement has evangelistic consequences as we bear witness to the transforming grace of Jesus Christ."[5]

Mission and Creation Care

At the same time as a more integral understanding of mission began to form, there was an increasing unpredictability in weather events and an increasing number of natural disasters. Scientists began pointing to the effects that anthropogenic and other greenhouse gas emissions were having on our climate, and the term "climate change" began to be used more frequently. The Intergovernmental Panel on Climate Change (IPCC), an intergovernmental body of the United Nations, defines climate change as "a change in the state of the climate that can be identified (e.g. using statistical tests) by changes in the mean and/or the variability of its properties, and that persists for an extended period, typically decades or longer. It refers to any change in climate over time, whether due to natural variability or as a result of human activity."[6]

---

3. Micah Global (www.micahnetwork.org) is a global Christian community of organizations and individuals committed to integral mission, currently with 626 members registered in 89 countries.

4. "We affirm that evangelism and socio-political involvement are both part of our Christian duty. . . . The salvation we claim should be transforming us in the totality of our personal and social responsibilities. Faith without works is dead" (Lausanne Movement, "Lausanne Covenant," Section 5).

5. Micah Network, "Integral Mission," 1.

6. UNFCCC, "Fact Sheet," 1.

As EFICOR and other organizations continued to work directly with impoverished communities, we saw the disruptive and harmful effects that climate change was having on the poor, who themselves contributed very little to the problem. It became clear to us that the environmental impact of a warming climate as well as the injustice of climate change demanded an urgent response from Christian organizations and churches. In 2009 the Micah Network presented the "Declaration on Creation Stewardship and Climate Change," which synthesized the findings of the Fourth Triennial Global Consultation held in Kenya. The Micah Network claimed that "[The Declaration] . . . may perhaps in time be regarded as the most significant document coming out of the evangelical movement on a subject that has hardly received in the past the attention it deserves from people who confess the triune God as the God of Creation."[7]

The awareness of the need for Christians to intentionally address creation care and its implications has continued to grow. The Lausanne Cape Town Commitment of 2010 states:

> The earth is the property of the God we claim to love and obey. We care for the earth, most simply, because it belongs to the one whom we call Lord. . . . If Jesus is Lord of all the earth, we cannot separate our relationship to Christ from how we act in relation to the earth. For to proclaim the gospel that says "Jesus is Lord" is to proclaim the gospel that includes the earth, since Christ's Lordship is over all creation. Creation care is thus a gospel issue within the Lordship of Christ.[8]

The "Jamaica Call to Action"[9] drafted in 2012 built on this commitment, confirming the importance and urgency of the matter. Having attended the Lausanne Cape Town Conference and been directly involved in the drafting of the Micah "Declaration" and the "Call to Action," it was obvious to me that the voices of people from all around the world needed to be heard. A deeper understanding of God, of his mission and of how we are to live as disciples of Christ was to be found not just in the halls of learning, but also through listening to the voices of his people.

7. Micah Network, "Creation Stewardship," 1.
8. Lausanne Movement, "Cape Town Commitment," I.7.A.
9. Lausanne Movement, "Creation Care and the Gospel."

The Challenges of Engaging the Church in Integral Mission

It has been great to see a more comprehensive understanding of mission slowly develop both in India and globally: one in which stewardship of the environment is included as a key component. It has also become clearer over time that it is necessary to address the root causes of many of the issues that are faced by communities across the globe: a lack of understanding of who owns the earth, and a limited and selective interpretation of what it means to love our neighbour.

Whose Earth?

Psalm 24:1 states, "The earth is the Lord's." In my interaction with many Christian groups I have found that people do not have any problem acknowledging God as the Creator God; in fact, this is common across many religious beliefs. In India, most Christians also do not interpret having "dominion" or "ruling over" the earth, as some biblical translations express it in Genesis 1–2, as a licence to use and abuse. What we do, however, fail to recognize and perhaps avoid is the question of who owns this world. God owns it and delights in it. The Genesis 1 account of the creation story shows clearly how delighted God is in his creation. God created human beings as divine image bearers, giving them the responsibility of caring for God's earth and all creatures. Being made in God's image is a job description given to humanity to practise servant-kingship, ruling and managing the rest of creation, and to do so in a way that reflects God's character. Creation is relational; we can see this in the task given to Adam of naming the beasts and the birds, and in the creation of a female co-worker to help tend the gardens. Before the entry of sin, this was the sacred ground in which God dwelled with his created people – a land in which he delighted.

Sadly, we have come to view land as a commodity that we own, as something to be used in ways that serve our individual needs. We have put up walls and fences to protect our private spaces and we have exploited the land in pursuit of profit. Fortunately, there are still communities in India and around the world which demonstrate a traditional and sustainable approach to the land. Many parts of India are dotted with "sacred groves," which are "forest fragments of varying sizes, which are communally protected, and which usually have a significant religious connotation for the protecting community. Hughes and Chandran (1998) defined sacred groves as 'segments of landscape, containing vegetation, life forms and geographical features, delimited and protected by human societies under the belief that to keep them in a relatively undisturbed state is an expression of an important relationship of humans with the divine or with nature.'"[10] The religious belief is that protecting these groves pleases the deity. These sacred groves are thus protected as a response of "fear" to the deity – fear that something evil might happen if anything, even a twig, is taken out of it. What a difference it would make if we, as Christians, acknowledged who the earth belonged to and responded, not in fear, but as an expression of our faith; if we were to tend and take care of the rest of creation because it is our God-given responsibility as the "crown of creation."

Loving Our Neighbour

It is on this one earth and one planet that we need to co-exist and live. In response to the question about which commandment in the law was the greatest, Jesus said, "'You shall love the Lord your God with all your heart, and with all your soul, and with all your mind.' This is the greatest and first commandment. And a second is like it: 'You shall love your neighbour as yourself'" (Matt 22:37–39). So what does it mean to love God and to love our neighbour?

EFICOR has been working among poor communities for over fifty years. In the last few years we have worked to rescue trafficked children and adults, who are often sold into slavery from their villages because their families can no longer produce enough to meet their needs. In a very simplistic way, if we ask what the root cause of this poverty is, could it be that the responsibility lies with forces much bigger than these individual families? In fact, is it our lack of care, our greed and our exploitation of the land that has caused this desperation, disease and death? Have some of us used the earth to feed our greed, resulting in others not even getting their basic needs met? According to Global Footprint Network, 29 July 2019 was the "Earth Overshoot Day . . . [which] marks the date when humanity's annual demand on nature exceeds what Earth's ecosystems can regenerate in that year . . . humanity is currently using nature 1.75 times faster than our planet's ecosystems can regenerate, equivalent to 1.75 Earths."[11] Taking individual data of countries, it is estimated that if we all lived like people in the US, it would take five earths to sustain us; if we lived like Australians, it would take four earths; and if we lived like people in India or Nepal, 0.7 earths.[12] Global consumption patterns clearly indicate that

---

10. Kharkongor and Tiwari, "Sacred Groves," 346; citing J. D. Hughes and M. D. S. Chandran, "Sacred Groves around the Earth: An Overview" (1998).

11. "Earth Overshoot Day 2020 Lands on August 22," www.overshootday.org.

12. Global Footprint Network, "National Footprint."

certain countries are consuming the earth's resources disproportionately. Even within countries, there is a huge gap in consumption of the earth's resources. How on God's earth can some consume so much that it would take five earths to sustain their lifestyles? Loving our neighbour requires that we realize that our consumption patterns impact and harm our neighbours who live on the other side of the world.

Realizing the Impact of Waste

Our disproportionate patterns of consumption have resulted in large-scale waste. When God created the world there was no waste; there was enough for everybody. Everything had a cycle and a season. Even our bodies, as part of the earth, will return to dust. The very water we consume has gone through millions of rounds of recycling through natural processes that God ordained in nature. But as time has gone by, and as countries have experienced times of wealth and prosperity, the level of waste has exploded.[13] The United Nations Food and Agriculture Organization estimates the world produces enough food waste – about 1.3 billion tonnes – to feed most of the world's hungry people each year.[14] That is roughly one-third of the global food supply. "In a world of 7 billion people, set to grow to 9 billion by 2050, wasting food makes no sense – economically, environmentally, and ethically," says Achim Steiner, UN Undersecretary General and UN Environment Programme executive director.[15] What does it mean to love the 925 million people who do not have enough to eat?

It is not just about food waste. Over the years we have progressed in areas of health, sanitation, transport and technology, and have manufactured a lot of items, particularly items that cannot just go back to the earth. Our non-biodegradable waste is choking God's earth. The landfill just outside Delhi where I live and work is now as tall as the Taj Mahal (73 m) – an iconic monument in India. Ragpickers, at great risk to their lives, sort through the waste, helping to reduce the waste that fills up landfills. Globally, we have recently been bombarded with images of plastic waste floating in the oceans and among wildlife. Ultimately, waste causes death. A 2019 report, "No Time to Waste" by Tearfund, Fauna & Flora International, WasteAid and the Institute of Development Studies, highlights the disastrous impact that plastic waste has

---

13. FAO, "Food Wastage."
14. FAO, "Think."
15. FAO.

on the environment and on those who contribute the least to the problem.[16] Who produces this waste, and who dies as a result of it?

In the West, waste is generated in huge amounts and yet is not visible. In the news we see stories of how conscientiously sorted recycled waste is shipped to other countries. As a result, mountains of mostly plastic waste – which is not, in fact, easily recyclable – lies in these countries far away from those who produced the waste in the first place.[17] What cannot be thrown in my backyard is now thrown in someone else's backyard. How do we love our neighbours in our waste-producing lives? Will we be held accountable for the waste we produce? The media publish interviews with grateful people who are working in the "waste" industries. Their argument is that jobs have been generated and children have been able to be educated as a result of waste dumping. The message behind this is, in short, "Thank you for dumping your waste on us." I am not sure Jesus would agree with this method of loving our neighbours.

Acknowledging the Climate Emergency

Another important issue that has ravaged nations is climate change – a much-debated and disputed topic in the USA, but the impact of which is actually being felt now in India through extreme weather events, changing monsoon patterns and record temperatures. EFICOR works with farmers who tell us the same story of how things have changed. Unpredictable monsoons, which come either too early or too late, and bring too much rain or too little, have consistently affected production. Changing weather patterns and more frequent droughts and flooding are causing huge losses for farmers and having a disastrous impact: "Based on data collected for over a decade, on an average 45 farmers committed suicide per day in India."[18] While environmental degradation and misuse of chemical fertilizers have contributed to the devastation farmers are experiencing, it is reported that climate change has acted as the last nail in the coffin. Climate change is not a matter of debate in India. We live it and have to adapt to it – it is a reality with which we have to wrestle in real, practical and immediate terms.

It is becoming evident that it is the poorest countries (and within them the poorest people) – which have produced the lowest carbon emissions,

---

16. Tearfund, "No Time to Waste." Additional resources on this topic may be accessed through Tearfund, "Waste Management," https://learn.tearfund.org/en/Themes/Environment%20and%20Climate/Waste%20Management/.

17. Tearfund, "Burning Question"; Tearfund, "No Time to Waste," 47.

18. DownToEarth, "45 Farmers."

and have least resilience to enable them to respond – that bear the brunt of climate-related disasters, desertification, droughts, floods and extreme temperatures.[19] With increasing disasters there will be increasing climate-related displacement – climate refugees. In this climate of change, how do we respond faithfully to the command to love our neighbour? By the time we finish arguing about climate change, many more farmers will have committed suicide in desperation.

Responding as the People of God

How must we respond as the people of God? Often, response is driven by fear: fear of the deity that compels people to protect "sacred groves," fear of climate disaster that compels people to look after the environment. While fear can be a driving factor, long-lasting behavioural change is rarely driven by fear. How must we respond as the people of God? The Lausanne Cape Town Commitment beautifully captures this:

> This love [of God's creation] is not mere sentimental affection for nature (which the Bible nowhere commands), still less is it pantheistic worship of nature (which the Bible expressly forbids). Rather it is the logical outworking of our love for God by caring for what belongs to him. "The earth is the Lord's and everything in it." The earth is the property of the God we claim to love and obey. We care for the earth, most simply, because it belongs to the one whom we call Lord. The earth is created, sustained and redeemed by Christ. We cannot claim to love God while abusing what belongs to Christ by right of creation, redemption and inheritance. We care for the earth and responsibly use its abundant resources, not according to the rationale of the secular world, but for the Lord's sake.[20]

Caring for God's world is part of our biblical calling and not an optional extra. In our journey of creating awareness we found that many institutionalized churches in India had an environment policy (e.g. the Church of South

---

19. Tearfund, "Dried Up, Drowned Out"; Lamtinhoi, "Coping with Climate Change."
20. Lausanne, "Cape Town Commitment," I.7.A.

India[21] and the National Council of Churches in India[22]) and are already doing extensive work. But for many other churches, it was the first time they realized what the Bible teaches about creation care. Many pastors and Christian leaders, on hearing creation care theology, become passionate advocates for responsible stewardship of the environment; they return home with many ideas of how they can motivate their communities to be better caretakers of the earth. Responding to climate change is a challenge for the church in India and in many other parts of the Global South, but to their credit these churches have not wasted time debating whether it is necessary to become involved.

Moving Away from Convenience

Many of us have sacrificed God's world at what I call the "altar of convenience." Once when I taught on the subject of creation care, one senior missionary said, "Sister, I agree with everything you say – the theology, what we need to do, how it harms the environment. The problem is, all these things are so convenient. It is very difficult to give them up." Unfortunately, this desire for convenience has been exploited by the capitalist market economy. Indigenous, local and environmentally friendly practices in India were steamrollered by markets that supplied cheap, easy, convenient, individually packaged goods; for example, shampoo that came in attractive plastic bottles became more appealing and convenient than natural hair-cleansing products. Companies became cleverer and started packaging everything in single-use plastic sachets, making their product accessible to a poorer person who could not afford to purchase a whole bottle. The church has been no exception. At church events we usually end up with a pile of discarded polystyrene plates, plastic cups, disposable cutlery and empty water bottles. These items all end up in the trash and we are thankful that no one has to wash up afterwards. Some church leaders have even confessed that they burned the discarded plates and cups, watching them melt and produce toxic fumes. In our training events we draw attention to how harmful and destructive it is to prioritize convenience over what is good for the environment. As a result, many of the participants in our teaching events have repented of their actions committed out of ignorance, and promised to

---

21. Church of South India, "Ecological Concerns: Aims & Objective," https://www.csisynod.com/erec.php.

22. The Commission on Justice, Peace and Creation (National Council of Churches in India), "Policy on Indian Churche's [sic] Engagement in Eco-justice Ministries," http://ncci1914.com/wp-content/uploads/2017/06/Policy-on-Eco-justice-Ministries-of-the-Indian-Churches.pdf.

change their behaviour in the future. We have even had church leaders writing letters of apology to future generations – a powerful exercise in acknowledging not only that this is God's world, but that loving our neighbour also includes showing care and consideration for future generations.

Look South?

We often look to the West, partly because it was through the West that we first heard the gospel. We sing your songs – whether they are old hymns or contemporary worship songs. Our people come and study in seminaries and Bible schools in your countries. There is a desire to live like you do. But is it time that you learned from nations like ours? Interestingly, many in the West are "discovering" our amazing indigenous practices and using them. Perhaps the fact that we have lived so harmoniously with the rest of creation has meant that we did not necessarily have to have specific teaching on creation care? Maybe my father's care for creation was an outworking of his faith which influenced all aspects of his life, and did not require a specific book or "word study" for justification.

What can we learn from the church in the West in relation to creation care? Will the church in the West remain so divided by the politics of climate change that it fails to acknowledge and respond to the impact of climate change being felt now around the world?

Conclusion: God's Ownership and Neighbour Love Lead to Action

"The earth is the LORD's and all that is in it" (Ps 24:1a): it has been a journey for me to learn what that means and what it means to love our neighbour in God's world. My understanding of God and his Word draws me into an ever-growing awe of his creation and of the depth of responsibility God has given to us as his image bearers. If I do not care for God's earth, I do not love God, nor do I love my neighbour. So what can we do about this?

One of the first things we can do is to *stop*:

- *Stop* wasting time arguing about whether creation care matters or not, whether climate change is real or not. The impact of climate change is being felt everywhere.
- *Stop* thinking that the earth belongs to you and you are free to do whatever you want with it. It belongs to God, so treat the earth as sacred.

- *Stop* and reflect on whether your understanding of God affects every part of your life on this earth.

What can we *start* doing?

- *Start* by acknowledging that the resources of this earth are for everyone to share. There is only one earth, not five!
- *Start* speaking up: loving our neighbours and living lives that look after the earth is not a political opinion, it is our faith. Educate and encourage others by using your voice.
- *Start* listening to people across the world whose forests are dry, whose air is polluted and whose rivers are choked as a result of having to manufacture products to feed our consumerist lifestyle or to absorb our waste.

In 2017, the snowy owl was categorized as a "vulnerable" species by the International Union for Conservation of Nature. Should it matter to us? God created all living beings. The earth belongs to God. We are commanded to love God and to love our neighbours. Why would it not matter to us?

References

DownToEarth. "45 Farmers Commit Suicide Each Day in India." 4 July 2015. https://www.downtoearth.org.in/news/45-farmers-commit-suicide-each-day-in-india--34387.

FAO (Food and Agriculture Organization of the United Nations). "Food Wastage Footprint: Impacts on Natural Resources." 2013. http://www.fao.org/3/i3347e/i3347e.pdf.

———. "Think, Eat, Save: FAO, UNEP and Partners Launch Global Campaign on Food Waste." 22 January 2012. http://www.fao.org/news/story/en/item/168515/icode/.

Global Footprint Network. "National Footprint and Biocapacity Accounts, 2019 Public Data Package." https://www.footprintnetwork.org/licenses/public-data-package-free/.

Kharkongor, B. M., and B. K. Tiwari. "Sacred Groves of Meghalaya: A Review." *International Journal of Science and Research* 6, no. 3 (2017): 346–349. https://ijsr.net/archive/v6i3/ART20171342.pdf.

Lamtinhoi, Hoinu Kipgen. "Coping with Climate Change: The Story of the Maltos of Jharkhand." *Economic and Political Weekly* 51, no. 52 (24 Dec. 2016). https://www.epw.in/journal/2016/52/perspectives/coping-climate-change.html.

Lausanne Movement. "The Cape Town Commitment." 2011. https://www.lausanne.org/content/ctcommitment#capetown.

————. "Creation Care and the Gospel: Jamaica Call to Action." 2012. https://www.lausanne.org/content/statement/creation-care-call-to-action.

————. "The Lausanne Covenant." 1974. https://www.lausanne.org/content/covenant/lausanne-covenant#cov.

Micah Network. "Declaration on Creation Stewardship and Climate Change." 2009. https://www.micahnetwork.org/sites/default/files/doc/resources/mn_declaration_on_creation_stewardship.pdf.

————. "Micah Network Declaration on Integral Mission." September 2001. http://www.micahnetwork.org/sites/default/files/doc/page/mn_integral_mission_declaration_en.pdf.

Tearfund. "The Burning Question: Will Companies Reduce Their Plastic Use?" 2020. https://learn.tearfund.org/~/media/files/tilz/circular_economy/2020-tearfund-the-burning-question-en.pdf.

————. "Dried Up, Drowned Out: Voices from Poor Communities on a Changing Climate." 2012. https://learn.tearfund.org/~/media/files/tilz/research/dried_up_drowned_out_2012_-_full_report.pdf.

————. "No Time to Waste: Tackling the Plastic Pollution Crisis before It's Too Late." 2019. https://learn.tearfund.org/~/media/files/tilz/circular_economy/2019-tearfund-consortium-no-time-to-waste-en.pdf?la=en.

UNFCCC (United Nations Framework Convention on Climate Change). "Fact Sheet: Climate Change Science – The Status of Climate Change Science Today." February 2011. https://unfccc.int/files/press/backgrounders/application/pdf/press_factsh_science.pdf.

8

Seeing God's World

Proximity and Political Ecology within the Lordship of Christ

Laura S. Meitzner Yoder

Introduction: Coming to See and to Bear Witness

In 2016, a colleague asked me what vision I would have for our community. At that time, I sought to interweave more earnestly some professional threads to make one cloth. One strand was environmental concerns, especially how the slow violence of exclusion and greed lead to resource degradation, eroding the lives and livelihoods of vulnerable people, particularly in places I knew well in South East Asia. Another was a commitment to learning from people who are directly affected by a given situation – local experts, authoritative on their own reality. A third was how interpretation and behaviour, regarding texts and circumstances, are influenced by our experience, culture and social location.

My reply to her question was that how we cared for God's world would bear witness to following Christ in loving God and neighbour. However, it is evident that we in the North American church are theologically hamstrung in this witness by cultural individualism, a predilection for dualism, sacralized consumption and addiction to comfort. I added that, given our own many limitations to enacting this vision, I hoped it could come about from our humble willingness to be led and discipled in building our frail theology and practice of environmental care by churches, leaders and communities of the Majority World. Her expansive question proved to be the seed of the symposium that produced this volume.

For John Stott, evidence of Christian commitment should be visible through the disciple's everyday actions and behaviour. In *The Radical Disciple*, he pointedly described the evasive human strategy: "Our common way of avoiding radical discipleship is to be selective: choosing those areas in which commitment suits us and staying away from those areas in which it will be costly. But because Jesus is Lord, we have no right to pick and choose the areas in which we will submit to his authority."[1] Ignoring creation care, or relegating it to the domain of those with natural interests, is one area of disobedience we practise and justify in all kinds of ways. For Stott, all disciples' obedience necessarily includes living in ways that reflect care for God's creation. Such care is preceded by attentiveness that leads to awareness and concern.

The central question addressed in this chapter is simple: "How do we see and recognize the effects of our impacts on God's world?" To consider this question, we'll look through three windows linked to my discipline of political ecology, which studies the political dimensions of human–nature interactions. Political ecologists bridge natural and social sciences to study why we believe and act as we do with regard to our environment. The three windows give framing insights from colonial environmental history, reflect on water and insularity in an isolated corner of Timor-Leste, and draw on Dr Sam Berry's understanding of John Stott's own mid-life process of coming to identify environmental concerns as integral to Christian discipleship.

Window 1: Environmental History

The first view on our central question "How do we see and recognize our environmental impact?" takes us to colonial environmental history. Much literature on the origins of Western environmentalism points to North American settlers' encounters with the so-called "wilderness" of this continent, from the mid nineteenth century onwards. But environmental historian Richard Grove points to European colonial scientists' experiences in tropical island outposts from the early seventeenth century as critical antecedents that prompted the growth of global ecological awareness and conservation practices. This case usefully reminds us that the process of coming to see often involves getting close to unfamiliar realities and a willingness to un-see what we expect to find.

As background, the early years of European imperial exploits were based around extraction of wild forest and mineral resources worldwide for the benefit of the European metropole. With the rise of science in the seventeenth

---

1. Stott, *Radical Disciple*, 15–16.

century, incipient European colonizers deployed scientists to sparsely populated tropical island outposts to classify and to assess flora, fauna and minerals for commercial potential. At that time, travel reports show that Europeans considered "the tropical world . . . to possess illimitable resources."[2] Seeing lush vegetation and towering rainforests that grew without much seasonal pause, and so many unfamiliar plants and animals, the colonizers believed that resources, seemingly free for their taking, were inexhaustible on these oceanic island "Edens." "This notion . . . took a long time to dispel, and was first questioned [empirically] on island colonies,"[3] including St Vincent, Tahiti, Tobago, St Helena and Mauritius.

In the eighteenth century, these islands became experimental laboratories. Undertaking colonial plantation and forestry enterprises that presumed no bounds, the scientists observed the localized impacts of their economic activities. On these islands as elsewhere, "capital intensive plantation agriculture [such as for cotton], based on slave labour, promoted very rapid environmental change [in] deforestation and subsequent soil erosion, flooding, gullying . . . and drying up of the streams and rivers."[4] Gradually the scientists' experiences and systematic, up-close observation of biophysical changes on the island landscapes transformed their perspectives. Prior conceptualizations gave way to an acute awareness of the ecological impact of human activities, including fragility, exhaustibility, and human potential to cause resource degradation. They saw in real time how their economic activities had environmental and social consequences, developing "understanding [of humans'] . . . environmental agency, including both destruction and restoration."[5] In the microcosmic islands' contained spaces where limitations were rapidly evident, they were able to perceive ecological relationships among forests, rainfall, species decline or extinction, drought and soil degradation – and their corresponding human impacts of acute resource shortages and famine.

As scientists developed theories of environmental change, they engaged colonial governments to "grapple with the environmental consequences of [their] economic systems"[6] through deliberate conservation and restoration. They established botanic gardens to convey the realities of the rapid environmental deterioration they observed to influential people in their home

2. Grove, "Culture of Islands."

3. Grove.

4. Grove.

5. Grove, *Green Imperialism*, 476.

6. Grove, 477.

societies. While the scientists became aware of the phenomena of species extinction and other tragedies, they found that utilitarian self-interest was more compelling to nudge colonial governments to conservation action: over-extraction and degradation would eliminate the economic utility of colonies, and soil erosion causing local poverty and famine could push colonial subjects to social unrest. With Dave Bookless of A Rocha, I wonder about us: "Why should we look after [God's earth]? Are there better reasons than self-interest?"[7]

Through proximity and close attention in an unfamiliar place, these scientists came to understand environmental change in ways that had not been evident to them in their familiar home contexts. Importantly, the scientists allowed the islands' residents' indigenous understandings of nature as inseparably interrelated with human beings to influence their nascent ecological theories. This receptivity allowed the scientists to grapple with their own persistent dualism that perpetually distinguished the phenomena before them, obscuring interactions and connections. They learned to bridge the human–nature divide pervading Western approaches.[8]

Whether in the seventeenth or the twenty-first century, we can be slow to see and to recognize the effects of our actions. Being proximate, and unhurried, can allow us to see, to recognize and to perceive change. As Katongole and Rice challenge us, on God's journey of cosmic reconciliation "we have to unlearn three things: speed, distance, and innocence."[9] And as those who live in new places for a time can attest, deliberate attentiveness and receptivity to learning in and from the unfamiliar eventually affects what one sees at home, too.

Window 2: Water and Insularity

Our second window comes from another tropical island: Timor, in South East Asia. Oecusse is an enclave district of the small nation of Timor-Leste, where I have been involved since doctoral work there in the early 2000s. Oecusse is located on Timor's north-west coast, its 815 km^2 geographically separated from the main eastern body of Timor-Leste and surrounded by Indonesian West Timor; Oecusse is a remnant enclave of persistent affiliation with the Portuguese when the surrounding regions were progressively claimed by the

---

7. Bookless, *Planetwise*, 119.

8. For a modern linguistic example: In my work throughout Asia, I collect local terms for "nature" and "environment." Few Asian languages even have a word for environment-without-people. The very concept of unpeopled nature is puzzling in much of the world, accompanying the more recent global export and circulation of Western environmental ideas.

9. Katongole and Rice, *Reconciling All Things*, 79.

Dutch. Most of Oecusse's 65,000 people are subsistence farmers who face annual food shortages. Oecusse is drought prone, and has the nation's lowest Human Development indicators for most metrics.

Oecusse's enclave status presents unique challenges. Since Timor-Leste's independence from Indonesian occupation (1975–1999), Oecusse has had a relatively "hard" international land border surrounding it, which means that political and administrative regulations impede the passage of people and goods in and out of Oecusse by land. This curtails trade and social relationships with the more populous region that surrounds Oecusse, Indonesian West Timor, where many Oecusse families have relatives. Residents feel the enforced isolation most acutely in the annual several-month hungry season which begins as the year ends, as little food comes through the border. The hard border limits Oecusse residents from reaching the eastern body of their country, complicating their access to central governance and to national markets for their livestock. Unable to travel the 70 km gap by land, sometimes Oecusse people have an overnight boat option to the capital, subject to the wave season and the boat's functionality. It is extremely difficult to get in or out; Oecusse is truly outstanding for its inaccessibility.

From 2002 to 2004, my husband and I lived in Oecusse's capital town, next to the several hundred United Nations Peacekeeping Forces. From 1999 until the UN left Oecusse in 2003, the UN ferried Indonesian bottled water to the enclave by helicopter to meet the UN personnel's drinking water needs: at least three 1.5 litre plastic bottles per person, per day; on a national scale in Timor-Leste, distribution just to UN staff created waste of over ten million bottles per year.[10] With no recycling facilities on Timor, what was not burned created a substantial volume of plastic waste, some of which was eventually flown by helicopter from Timor to Australia for recycling (adding greatly to the carbon pollution cost of this bottled water). Those bottles have an estimated life expectancy of five hundred years, and they have already adorned the Timorese beaches for the past twenty.[11] But more troubling, perhaps, than the substantial plastic waste of this system was how it removed Oecusse town's critical lack of piped water – as the town's water system was destroyed during Indonesian-backed militia violence in 1999 – from being of central concern to

---

10. Laʼo Hamutuk, "UNTAET Bottled Water," 9. A pilot told me that the transport cost for the UN helicopters was more than US$10,000 per hour.

11. To learn more about single-use plastics, follow Tearfund's "Rubbish Campaign" in the UK (https://www.tearfund.org/en/about_you/action/rubbish/), in which churches and individuals seek to hold producers accountable for their plastic packaging, which ends up in God's oceans with branding intact.

the UN's transitional administration. I am reminded of how several regions of India banned bottled water so that visiting officials would be forced to become aware of the water shortages residents faced every day. A small fraction of the cost spent flying water and then empty bottles among three countries could have provided UN personnel *and* local residents *and* future inhabitants with a critical and basic human need. This was a tragically missed opportunity to support the common good. Municipal piped water still remains inadequate in Oecusse today, as we will see below.

In 2013, I was in Oecusse and attended a large public meeting led by a visiting top national official. He declared that the enclave would henceforth be a Special Economic Zone, unveiling a coastal development plan with a price tag of US$4.11 billion.[12] The first third of that sum was to be self-funded by the Timorese government, out of recently available petroleum revenues. The goal was to provide "basic infrastructure" (water, electricity, roads) to a few square kilometres of Oecusse's coastal capital town, hoping to attract foreign investment to the enclave which would generate income for the nation. International consultants drafted development plans. The government widely publicized one plan on posters dotting the seafront around Oecusse's capital town. Its contents surprised many Oecusse residents, including those whose neighbourhood was shown to house an industrial plant on their coral reef. The plan also featured two coastal resorts, with the larger resort adjacent to Oecusse's central river featuring a luxury hotel, water park and a twenty-seven-hole golf course – land uses requiring a significant water supply. This planned resort was overlaid on one of the two major reliable rice-producing areas of the district; rice paddy fields owned by individual families were visible around the overlaid edges of the resort on the posters. Much of the capital-intensive infrastructure (not the resorts) has now been built. Recently, a comprehensive World Bank study of this development plan deemed it not feasible; the consultants attempted to reach Oecusse by land, and their report chronicles their frustrated journey. And Oecusse town still does not have reliably running water.

One of the plan's major projects was to build an airport and runway large enough for jumbo jets. For this, the town's primary coastal forest, where people had grazed animals, found tamarind seeds to eat in the hungry season and gathered palm leaves to thatch their homes, was fenced off and cleared bare of all vegetation. The chief user of the luxurious airport is the regional government's own nineteen-passenger Twin Otter plane that flies to the capital,

---

12. Meitzner Yoder, "Development Eraser."

a one-way trip costing two months of a good local salary – for those few who have cash salaries at all. This $7 million plane is the transport equivalent of the bottled water: conveniently airborne, officials and the few people (mostly outsiders) who can afford to fly never need to notice the extreme hardship on Oecusse people from the hard border's limitations on local livelihoods and sustenance. Passengers need not lament that the plane's smooth landing cost a forest commons that had sustained hundreds of people. Missiologist Jon Bonk writes: "the primary advantage of wealth lies in its capacity to provide goods and services that cushion the wealthy from the harsh vicissitudes of poverty."[13] We "often inhabit islands in seas of poverty. [Our] affluence quite literally constitutes the 'nonconducting material' that shields [us] from the 'heat' and 'sound' of that poverty which is the everyday experience" of people around us.[14] Our ordinary things, water bottles and aeroplanes, keep us from being close enough to see, to know, to feel and to care.

This insulating effect struck me in a new way in late 2015, when the national government held a celebration of five hundred years of Portuguese presence in Timor-Leste. Oecusse, site of the first Portuguese landing, became host to many dignitaries from Portuguese-speaking countries and the Catholic Church. Pop-up restaurants along the beach appeared for the week, selling high-end imported foods and drinks, and Australian meat and produce, marvels never before seen in Oecusse. I overheard two visitors discussing how, despite Oecusse's reputation for being really backward and rustic, it sure seemed to have all the amenities of any major city, and such great sunsets. Visitors' cars that had arrived effortlessly by land from the national capital in a special motorcade were washed of dust throughout the day. Meanwhile, not far from the short-lived restaurants, Oecusse residents stood in long lines overnight for weeks, waiting their turn to fill their kitchen containers with water dripping from a public standpipe.

This 2015 event brought into relief the extent and impacts of the blinding effects of the cushion of privilege. The event enabled two disparate realities to co-exist, undisturbed by their proximity. I had lived in Oecusse for years, and knew the normal challenges of life there. Before 2015, nearly everyone in the district was in the same situation. No one had sufficient steady piped water, and when the food ran out, we all had much less to eat until harvest-time in a few months. But in 2015, the short-term visitors feasted on imported delicacies, so easily unaware that local food had been commandeered to feed the district's

---

13. Bonk, *Missions and Money*, 53.

14. Bonk, 54.

guests. As for the guests: stomach full, one need look no further than one's own plate. Water bottle in hand, one doesn't notice that the village tap next door has run dry. Walking by the pop-up restaurants en route to my friends' home where I was staying, in a neighbourhood where some local parents were putting their kids to bed hungry, Matthew 25 came to mind in relation to water in this island enclave. When did we see your beaches ankle-deep in our water bottles, and you wading through them to wash your dishes in the ocean because no water ran at home? When did we see your river diverted to create playgrounds for foreigners built on top of your only rice field? When did we see you standing in line overnight for water? These questions are claims that we have *not* seen. Blindness, caused by our carefully maintained distance, and by being unaffected.

How do we see and recognize the effects of our impacts on God's world?

Window 3: John Stott's Concern for Creation Care

This brings us back to Stott, and to our third window. Here I draw on an as-yet-unpublished manuscript,[15] which came to my attention in 2017 via Ed Brown of the Lausanne/World Evangelical Alliance Creation Care Network. Since 2013, some of John Stott's closest friends and colleagues had encouraged Dr Sam Berry, an eminent British scientist and founding member of the A Rocha Council of Reference (with Stott), as he collected and interpreted Stott's various writings, sermons and statements on environment and creation care. At Sam Berry's passing, he left a nearly completed manuscript. In 2018, I met with Sam's widow, Dr Caroline Berry, and she passed this project to me to carry forward as possible.

In Stott's farewell to the worldwide church, his final book includes "the care of our created environment" as one of the eight characteristics of committed Christian discipleship.[16] To some, such a statement is confusing or troubling, theologically or otherwise. It does not align with what we may have learned or lived for decades in church and Christian community. Creation care is conspicuous in the church chiefly by our studious and sometimes sophisticated neglect of it.

Calling environmental care "an integral part of the mission of the Church and a challenge for all Christians," writes Berry, "seems eccentric, even startling. Most Christians [may] agree that creation care is commendable and should

---

15. Berry, "Stott on the Environment."
16. Stott, *Radical Disciple*, 49.

be encouraged, but would be unlikely to rate it as a required discipline for all believers. For [some] evangelicals in particular, earth tends to be regarded as little more than a theatre for salvation, a preparation for eternal life elsewhere."[17] So why would serious Christ-followers bother with it? Perhaps Stott is just overstating; we may want to blame or dismiss his confusing penchant for creation care on his active birdwatching; maybe he sought to justify his hobby. How did Stott come to see the spiritual importance of our impacts on God's world? Here we consider the background to his commitment, and what we can learn from the implications.

Stott concludes his creation care chapter in *The Radical Disciple* with reference to Chris Wright's desire to see "a growing number of Christians who 'include the care of creation within their biblical concept of mission,'"[18] citing from Wright's book *The Mission of God*: "It seems quite inexplicable to me that there are some Christians who claim to love and worship God, to be disciples of Jesus and yet have no concern for the earth that bears his stamp of ownership. They do not care about the abuse of the earth, and indeed by their wasteful and over-consumptive life-styles they collude in it."[19] Stott continues: "God intends . . . our care of the creation to reflect our love for the Creator."[20] For Stott, this is why it matters.

Not surprising is Stott's firm focus on "the need for theological commitment. . . . His approach is unapologetically biblical. It begins with creation involving the nature of humankind in God's image, continues with human disobedience . . . and concludes with God's restoring work in repairing the broken relationships we have with God, each other, and the creation itself."[21]

We may see the world as ours. Psalm 24 reminds us that it is not. Unlike our Creator God, we rush through the first five days of created goodness, failing to marvel at stars, water, plants, fish, birds, all declared good apart from their usefulness to humanity. We refuse to pause, to observe, and to be humbled by divine creativity. We can be so self-centred and impatient, racing past the rest of God's good world in our headlong rush to feature ourselves. We not only fail to appreciate; we are active extinguishers of our God's good creativity. Stott notes that we should avoid both deifying nature and exploiting it to

---

17. Berry, "Stott on the Environment."
18. Stott, *Radical Disciple*, 58.
19. Wright, *Mission of God*, 414.
20. Stott, *Radical Disciple*, 59.
21. Berry, "Stott on the Environment."

destruction, instead following the better way of cooperating with God.[22] This is our "role – part of our God-given mission [and God's original intention for humanity]. . . . Stott's approach turns the common approach for caring for the environment on its head: it begins with God, not human misdemeanours."[23]

As Berry notes, "Stott insisted on a number of occasions [that] Christians have a much weaker doctrine of creation than of redemption. Stott deplored this imbalance, seeing it as producing an [unbiblical Enlightenment] dualism between spirit and matter *that was an effect of the Fall*, [a separation] which is countermanded throughout the scriptures."[24] He believed that such dichotomizing showed how "we have imported into our thinking distinctions and rankings that do not really reflect the wholeness of the biblical worldview and teaching. We insist on taxonomies where the Bible calls for simple obedience to the totality of its mandates on the lives of God's people – or in Jesus' simpler words, 'to obey all that I have commanded you.'"[25]

Stott's growth into integral mission (proclaiming the gospel in word together with social action) shows that he believed that such action and evangelism were improperly separated. Their contentious integration became a hallmark of the 1974 Lausanne Covenant, which Stott drafted. Looking back, he was decades ahead of his time for the Western church in understanding and embracing integral mission, and, as we will also see, on environmental concern.

How, and when, did Stott come to this strength of conclusion? I find it striking that it was in the late 1960s, from Stott's late forties and during his fifties, that he developed some of the theological commitments for which he later became best known. Let us look first at Stott's growing understanding of what we today call "integral mission," the term *misión integral* which accompanied the theological leadership on this point from Latin American theologians with whom Stott interacted in these years.

Reflecting on how his own 1966 World Congress on Evangelism teaching about the Great Commission did *not* include social responsibility, Stott said he was relieved that his own Bible studies there were not widely distributed. He said, "I now consider that I was unbalanced to assert that the risen Lord's commission was entirely evangelistic, not social . . . I later argued that at least the Johannine version of the Commission (with its words 'as the Father sent me, so I send you') implies in us as in Christ a ministry of compassionate service that is

---

22. Stott, *Radical Disciple*, 52–53.
23. Berry, "Stott on the Environment."
24. Berry.
25. Berry.

wider than evangelism."[26] Eight years later, in 1974, his drafting of the Lausanne Covenant (at the age of fifty-three) made evident his coalescing support of integral mission, which was rare among Euro-American evangelicals at that time, and to some degree even today. After decades of scriptural immersion, what caused this shift in Stott's thinking with regard to integral mission?

In a 1989 interview (at the age of sixty-eight), Stott reflected on the reasons for his change of mind, saying it came about

> gradually, and I don't think it was through anybody's particular influence but through my own reflection on the New Testament, I came to see that this view was very narrow and unbiblical. In the early 1960s, I began to travel in the Third World, and I saw poverty in Latin America, Africa and Asia as I had not seen it before. It became clear to me that it was utterly impossible to take that old view. Since then I have come to a much more holistic position.[27]

Stott was well known as an advocate of "double listening" to the Word and to the world, the Bible and the newspaper held in tandem, thinking deeply and biblically on the problems of modern society, without conforming to contemporary fashion. But his explanation does not mention being convinced by new scientific knowledge or keeping up with the current times – though Stott clearly sought to engage with cutting-edge science and a wide range of contemporary issues. He notes two influences: first, biblical study; and second, direct, proximate interactions with people and places deeply affected by poverty. In the case of his growing understanding of creation care around those same years, much of Stott's study focused on Psalms 103–104. This led him to refuse to separate God's work in creation from that in redemption, a theme he revisited and strengthened over decades especially around these psalms. Here again, Stott turns the usual approach to caring for the environment on its head: this time, since "God intends . . . our care of the creation to reflect our love for the Creator," creation care is not a distraction from the main work of the church, but it is properly central to the life, identity and mission of the church, essential to discipleship for all Christians. Remarkably for a leader of his stature, Stott expressed a humble willingness to change his mind if he became convinced that his own biblical interpretation was in error.

Stott's contributions and engagements on Christian environmental concern grew quickly from the 1970s onwards, evidenced in his preaching, writing,

---

26. Dudley-Smith, *Global Ministry*, 123.
27. Dudley-Smith, 127.

educational initiatives and institutional commitments. Peter Harris, co-founder of A Rocha, commented, "When I first met John in the late 1970s, he was already thinking deeply about how the care of creation . . . integrated with discipleship and mission. By . . . 1993 he was even ahead of our own thinking in his understanding from Psalms 19 and 104 and elsewhere that the creation, 'the works of the Lord,' were themselves to be understood as an integral element in 'the glory of the Lord.'"[28] The following list illustrates Stott's increasing attention to creation care:[29]

- 1977: All Souls sermon on "God and the Environment," largely an exposition of Psalm 104.
- 1980: "An Evangelical Commitment to Simple Lifestyle" (Lausanne Occasional Paper #20); conference co-chair, with Ron Sider.
- 1982: Founded the London Institute for Contemporary Christianity (LICC): every part of our lives comes under the lordship of Christ, and all of life is a context for worship, mission, ministry and active Christian engagement.
- 1983: Member of the International Council of Reference for the newly founded A Rocha, established as an organization for "Christians in Conservation," and served in this capacity to the end of his life.
- 1983–1997: President of Tearfund, engaging Christians to respond to the multiple dimensions contributing to poverty, including environmental degradation.
- 1984: *Issues Facing Christians Today* published, with a chapter on "Our Human Environment" (becomes "Caring for Creation" in later editions).
- 1985: Organizes joint conference of LICC and Christian Ecology Group on "People, Technology and the Environment."
- 1990: Study pack "Green Issues" produced by LICC, with succinct paper by Stott on "the biblical imperative for conservation."
- 1994: Endorses the "Evangelical Declaration on the Care of Creation" drafted by the Theological Commission of the World Evangelical Fellowship as a response to the WCC Consultation on "Justice, Peace and the Integrity of Creation"; writes Foreword to *The Care of Creation* (2000) produced as a commentary on the Declaration.

---

28. Personal communication, 25 September 2019.
29. Much of this list is found in Berry, "Stott on the Environment."

- 1999: *The Birds Our Teachers* published.
- 2010: Stott endorsed the Cape Town Commitment's going beyond the integration of only the two spheres of evangelism and social concern to embrace creation care as well.
- 2010: *The Radical Disciple* published, with "Creation Care" as one of the marks of Christian discipleship.

Looking Forward: Majority World Voices in Creation Care

In accord with Stott, many Christian scholars worldwide agree that we have an underdeveloped theology of creation. There is much scope for leadership by Majority World scholars and communities in this area. As with the eighteenth-century scientists, a cultural overfondness for discrete classification and dualism may limit North Atlantic theological imaginations, and keep us from seeing integration and wholeness, *misión integral* and *shalom*. Like those scientists, people with different perspectives on what constitutes forests and trees may point the way forward. Are we able to listen, and willing to be taught, by those closest to the effects of our global environmental degradation? And are we close enough to do so? Are we aware of what insulates and isolates us, and of how to overcome that?

Ecology reminds us that our lives are bound up with one another. Observing global ecological interrelationships, we can no longer plead ignorance of how high-consumption lifestyles harm God's world and our neighbours. Political ecology situates these relationships in networks of power and resources, and reminds us that there are those who can afford to ignore the environmental degradation we cause, and those who cannot. Those of us who can literally *afford* to ignore contamination of land and water, extreme floods, and new realities of forests and oceans are rarely able to see, or rarely choose to know, the impacts on people who live in the midst of those circumstances.

A necessary step is to reframe creation care in ways that foreground responses and priorities of people in the Majority World, as well as indigenous people and communities of colour who suffer the greatest harm from environmental degradation. Several years ago, I was looking for Majority World authors on creation care and Christian environmental responsibility for a course reader, and found very little. I asked the twenty or so scholar-practitioner colleagues worldwide who I thought might have such a compilation. Some sent their own short bibliographies, but most replied that they didn't have an extensive collection either, and were similarly seeking such a resource list. Several individuals in linked organizations then joined efforts to develop a living bibliography and to make it available through Micah Global and other venues. The INFEMIT (International Fellowship of Mission as Transformation) network of Christian scholar-theologians in Africa, Asia, the Middle East and Latin America may read, select and recommend resources on the list as needed.

There is still much more scope for the church to work in this arena. For example, Tearfund is inviting local pastors in the Caribbean to give sermons on creation care themes, which are then collected with the goal of producing local language resources on creation care that actually fit the context of the local churches; the typical North Atlantic creation care admonitions to reduce air-conditioning, downsize one's car, go outside once in a while and eat less meat are not relevant for many Majority World congregations. Rural churches of people who live and make their living in direct contact with land and forests have first-hand knowledge of climate change impacts as well as the socio-political and biophysical challenges of land and forest care. What does taking care of God's earth look like in such settings and in their daily interactions with soil, land, water and creatures? What kinds of insights on our Creator God's original intentions for us and the rest of God's world will these sisters and brothers teach the church worldwide?

References

Berry, Sam. "Stott on the Environment." Unpublished manuscript.

Bonk, Jonathan J. *Missions and Money: Affluence as a Missionary Program Revisited.* Rev. and expanded ed. Maryknoll, NY: Orbis, 2006.

Bookless, Dave, *Planetwise: Dare to Care for God's World.* Nottingham: Inter-Varsity Press, 2008.

Dudley-Smith, Timothy. *John Stott: A Global Ministry.* Leicester: Inter-Varsity Press, 2001.

Grove, Richard H. "The Culture of Islands and the History of Environmental Concern." Harvard Seminar on Environmental Values. 18 April 2000. http://ecoethics.net/hsev/200004txt.htm.

————. *Green Imperialism: Colonial Expansion, Tropical Island Edens and the Origins of Environmentalism, 1600–1860.* Cambridge: Cambridge University Press, 1995.

Katongole, Emmanuel, and Chris Rice. *Reconciling All Things: A Christian Vision for Justice, Peace and Healing.* Downers Grove, IL: InterVarsity Press, 2008.

Laʾo Hamutuk. "UNTAET Bottled Water Facts (FY 2001)." *The Laʾo Hamutuk Bulletin* 2, no. 1 & 2, part 1 (Apr. 2001): 9. https://www.laohamutuk.org/Bulletin/2001/Apr/LHBl2n1E.pdf.

Meitzner Yoder, Laura S. "The Development Eraser: Fantastical Schemes, Aspirational Distractions and High Modern Mega-Events in the Oecusse Enclave, Timor Leste." *Journal of Political Ecology* 22 (2015): 299–321.

Stott, John. *The Radical Disciple: Some Neglected Aspects of Our Calling.* Downers Grove, IL: InterVarsity Press, 2010.

Wright, Christopher J. H. *The Mission of God: Unlocking the Bible's Grand Narrative.* Downers Grove, IL: InterVarsity Press, 2006.

List of Contributors

Dr. **Ruth Padilla DeBorst** serves with Resonate Global Mission, leading the Comunidad de Estudios Teológicos Interdisciplinarios (CETI), the International Fellowship for Mission as Transformation (INFEMIT), and leadership development initiatives of the Christian Reformed Church. She and her husband, James, are members of Casa Adobe, an intentional Christian community in Cost Rica concerned about living in right relations as part of the creation community. She has an MA in Interdisciplinary Studies from Wheaton College and a PhD in Theology from Boston University.

Mr. **Jason Fileta** serves as the Vice President of Tearfund USA. An author, speaker, and editor, Mr. Fileta was also the Director of the Micah Challenge USA. He has a BA in Sociology and International Development from Calvin College.

Dr. **Mark Labberton** serves as the President of Fuller Theological Seminary and was the Chair of John Stott Ministries (now Langham Partnership USA). An author, speaker, and teacher, Dr. Labberton has spent over thirty years in ministry searching out justice, love, and grace at the intersection between the academy, church, and culture. He has an MDiv from Fuller and a PhD in Theology from Cambridge University.

The Rt. Rev. Dr. **David Zac Niringiye** serves as a Senior Fellow at the Institute of Religion, Faith, and Culture in Public Live (INTERFACE). An author, pastor, and theologian, Bishop Zac works as a civic-political activist in Uganda, where he mobilizes young adults and others in civil society-led social justice and peace campaigns. He has an MA in Systematic Theology from Wheaton College and a PhD in Theology and Mission History from Edinburgh University.

Ms. **Lalbiakhlui "Kuki" Rokhum** serves as the Director of Training and Mobilization with the Evangelical Fellowship of India Commission on Relief (EFICOR). Ms. Rokhum focuses on seeking solutions to issues of justice by working with the poor and marginalized. She has a BA in Intercultural and Biblical Studies from All Nations Christian College.

Dr. **Myrto Theocharous** serves as a professor of Old Testament at Greek Bible College. An author and teacher, Dr. Theocharous trains Christian leaders in Greece. She has a MA in Biblical Exegesis from Wheaton College and a doctorate in Hebrew Studies from Cambridge University.

Dr. **Ruth Valerio** serves as Global Advocacy and Influencing Director for Tearfund UK. A speaker, author, social activist, and environmentalist, Dr. Valerio writes on justice, environment, and lifestyle. She has a PhD from Kings College London on simplicity and consumerism. She is also Canon Theologian at Rochester Cathedral.

Rev. Dr. **Christopher J. H. Wright** serves as International Ministries Director of Langham Partnership, founded by John Stott. An author, ordained pastor, and teacher, Dr. Wright has also worked as the chair of the Lausanne Theology Working Group and Academic Dean and Principal of All Nations Christian College. He has a PhD in Old Testament Economic Ethics from Cambridge University.

Dr. **Laura S. Meitzner Yoder** serves as John Stott Endowed Chair and Director of Human Needs and Global Resources, and Professor of Environmental Studies, at Wheaton College, Illinois. She advocates for smallholder farmers and forest dwellers, especially in Southeast Asia and Latin America. She has a PhD in Forestry and Environmental Studies from Yale University.

Langham Literature and its imprints are a ministry of Langham Partnership.

Langham Partnership is a global fellowship working in pursuit of the vision God entrusted to its founder John Stott –

to facilitate the growth of the church in maturity and Christ-likeness through raising the standards of biblical preaching and teaching.

Our vision is to see churches in the Majority World equipped for mission and growing to maturity in Christ through the ministry of pastors and leaders who believe, teach and live by the word of God.

Our mission is to strengthen the ministry of the word of God through:
- nurturing national movements for biblical preaching
- fostering the creation and distribution of evangelical literature
- enhancing evangelical theological education

especially in countries where churches are under-resourced.

Our ministry

Langham Preaching partners with national leaders to nurture indigenous biblical preaching movements for pastors and lay preachers all around the world. With the support of a team of trainers from many countries, a multi-level programme of seminars provides practical training, and is followed by a programme for training local facilitators. Local preachers' groups and national and regional networks ensure continuity and ongoing development, seeking to build vigorous movements committed to Bible exposition.

Langham Literature provides Majority World preachers, scholars and seminary libraries with evangelical books and electronic resources through publishing and distribution, grants and discounts. The programme also fosters the creation of indigenous evangelical books in many languages, through writer's grants, strengthening local evangelical publishing houses, and investment in major regional literature projects, such as one volume Bible commentaries like *The Africa Bible Commentary* and *The South Asia Bible Commentary*.

Langham Scholars provides financial support for evangelical doctoral students from the Majority World so that, when they return home, they may train pastors and other Christian leaders with sound, biblical and theological teaching. This programme equips those who equip others. Langham Scholars also works in partnership with Majority World seminaries in strengthening evangelical theological education. A growing number of Langham Scholars study in high quality doctoral programmes in the Majority World itself. As well as teaching the next generation of pastors, graduated Langham Scholars exercise significant influence through their writing and leadership.

To learn more about Langham Partnership and the work we do visit **langham.org**